SEEING AND SAVORING

JESUS CHRIST

S EEING AND S AVORING

JESUS
CHRIST

JOHN PIPER

CROSSWAY BOOKS • WHEATON, ILLINOIS
A DIVISION OF GOOD NEWS PUBLISHERS

Seeing and Savoring Jesus Christ

Copyright © 2001 by John Piper

Published by Crossway Books
       A division of Good News Publishers
       1300 Crescent Street
       Wheaton, Illinois 60187

Cover design: Cindy Kiple

Unless otherwise indicated, Bible quotations are taken from *The New American Standard Bible,* updated edition (1995), copyright © 1960, 1962, 1963, 1968, 1971, 1972, 1975, 1977, 1995 by The Lockman Foundation, and are used by permission.

Bible quotations marked RSV are taken from the *Revised Standard Version,* NIV from the *New International Version,* and NKJV from the *New King James Version.*

Note: Key words and phrases in Scripture quotations have been distinguished by italics (roman type in all-italics block quotations).

First printing, 2001

Printed in the United States of America

Library of Congress Cataloging-in-Publication Data
Piper, John, 1946-
  Seeing and savoring Jesus Christ / John Piper.
    p.   cm.
  Includes bibliographical references and indexes.
  ISBN 1-58134-265-9 (hardcover : alk. paper)
    1. Jesus Christ—Person and offices. 2. Glory of God. I. Title.
BT205.P58   2001
232'.8—dc21   2001000452
                                               CIP

15	14	13	12	11	10	09	08	07	06	05	04	03	02	01
15	14	13	12	11	10	9	8	7	6	5	4	3	2	1

To the memory of

C. S. Lewis
and Clyde Kilby

who taught me there is always
more to see in what I see

Contents

Acknowledgments

I owe the writing of this book to Jesus Christ. He died in my place, the righteous for the unrighteous. God counted him, who was sinless, to be a sinner, so that in him I, who am a sinner, could be counted righteous. He opened the blind eyes of my heart and brought me to faith and repentance. By his Spirit he has come to live in my heart through faith, and is slowly working his character into my stubborn will. Not only that, but this Jesus Christ created the world, including me, and holds it in being by the word of his power. Every breath I take, every beat of my heart, every moment of seeing and hearing, every movement of my mind, is owing to the sustaining grace and creative power of Jesus. All other acknowledgments and thanks are secondary and dependent on this one.

A special thanks to Bob Putman whose initiative encouraged me to write ten of these chapters as articles in *The Standard*. Thanks to Justin Taylor who gave them a careful reading and made helpful suggestions. Thanks to Ted Griffin who shepherded them gently through the press at Crossway. Thanks to Carol Steinbach for the indexes. And thanks to Noël who stands by my side in seeing and savoring Jesus. I am so glad that we see him together and that, at another level, you see in the editing process what I can't. The lines have fallen for me in pleasant places. I am surrounded with gracious and gifted people.

I pray that these brief chapters will become windows onto the panorama of the perfections of Jesus Christ. Everyone who shares in this project prays the same. May God grant you, the reader, to see Jesus Christ for who he really is and to savor him deeply with your soul's delight.

PREFACE

How Can We Be Sure About Jesus?

✧

In the middle of the last century the British writer C. S. Lewis got it shockingly right:

> A man who was merely a man and said the sort of things Jesus said would not be a great moral teacher. He would either be a lunatic—on the level with the man who says he is a poached egg—or else he would be the Devil of Hell. You can shut Him up for a fool, you can spit at Him and kill Him as a demon; or you can fall at His feet and call Him Lord and God. But let us not come with any patronizing nonsense about His being a great human teacher. He has not left that open to us. He did not intend to.[1]

In other words, Jesus will not be domesticated. But people still try. There seems to be something about this man for everybody. So we pick and choose in a way that shows he is on our side. All over the world, having Jesus on your side is a good thing. But not the original, undomesticated, unadjusted

Jesus. Just the revised Jesus who fits our religion or political platform or lifestyle.

When I was in graduate school in Germany in the 1970s, I reviewed a book called *Jesus für Atheisten*,[2] which you don't need German to translate. It was a Marxist "reading" of the life of Jesus. According to that book, the essence of Jesus' teaching was the call to radical action against the establishment. It was a call to ultimate devotion to "the kingdom"—the inbreaking of the new society (Marxism).

It is a strange thing that, among folks who do not follow Jesus as their Lord and God, almost no one wants to say bad things about him. The same thing is true of crosses: They are nice to wear for jewelry, but nobody wants to die on one. The only crosses people want are domesticated ones. It makes sense, then, that a man who calculated his whole life to die on one would be dangerous to believe in.

Can we know him as he really was—and is? How do we come to know a person who lived on the earth two thousand years ago—one who claimed to rise from the dead with indestructible life and therefore lives today? Some people say you can't. The real Jesus is buried in history, they say, and there is no access to him. Others are not so skeptical. They believe that the biblical records of Jesus' life are reliable, and that its earliest interpreters—like the apostle Paul—are more dependable guides than today's critics.

But how can you be sure that the biblical portrait of Jesus is true? People take two paths in search of solid ground under the feet of faith. One is the path of painstaking historical research to test the authenticity of the historical records. I followed this path during my formative years in seminary and graduate school and college teaching. In spite of all the challenges to my faith in those days, I was never shaken loose from the conviction that there is good warrant for trusting the New Testament documents about Jesus. Today there are many compelling books—both scholarly and popular—that support this confidence.[3]

But now I am a pastor rather than a college teacher. I still value the path of scholarly historical research. In fact, I lean on it often. However, I am more immediately aware now that the vast majority of people in the world will never have the time or the tools to trace out all the evidences for the historical reliability of the New Testament. If Jesus is the Son of God, if he died for our sins and rose from the dead, and if God meant for people, two thousand years later, to have a well-founded faith, then there must be another path to know the real Jesus, other than by rigorous, academic, historical research.

There is another path. It's the path I am following in this book. It starts with the conviction that divine truth can be self-authenticating. In fact, it would seem strange if God revealed himself in his Son Jesus Christ and inspired the record of that revelation in the Bible, but did not provide a way for ordinary people to know it. Stated most simply, the common path to sure knowledge of the real Jesus is this: Jesus, as he is revealed in the Bible, has a glory—an excellence, a spiritual beauty—that can be seen as self-evidently true. It is like seeing the sun and knowing that it is light and not dark, or like tasting honey and knowing that it is sweet and not sour. There is no long chain of reasoning from premises to conclusions. There is a direct apprehension that this person is true and his glory is the glory of God.

The apostle Paul described this path to knowledge of Jesus in 2 Corinthians 4:4-6:

> The god of this world has blinded the minds of the unbelieving so that they might not see *the light of the gospel of the glory of Christ, who is the image of God.* . . . For God, who said, "Light shall shine out of darkness," is the One who has shone in our hearts to give *the Light of the knowledge of the glory of God in the face of Christ.*

Notice that Paul speaks of God's enlightening our hearts (as in the work of creation) to apprehend "the knowledge of the glory of God in the face of Christ." He is talking about people who have never seen the historical Jesus. How can they know him and be sure of him? What they "see" is the verbal portrayal of Jesus in the Gospel, that is, in the apostolic preaching of Christ. This portrayal, Paul says, accompanied by God's shining "in our hearts," appears to us as what it really is—"the glory of God in . . . Christ," or as "the glory of Christ . . . the image of God."

You can see that two things make this path possible. One is the reality of the glory of Jesus Christ shining though his portrayal in the Bible. The other is the work of God to open the eyes of our blinded hearts to see this glory. This is very different from God "telling us" that the Bible is true. It is, rather,

God's enabling us to see what is really there. This is an important difference. If God whispered in our ear, as it were, that the Jesus of the Bible is true, then the whispering would have the final authority and everything would hang on that. But that is not the path I see in the Bible nor the path I follow. Rather Jesus himself, and his divinely inspired portrayal in the Bible, have the final authority.

The practical effect of this path is that I do not ask you to pray for a special whisper from God to decide if Jesus is real. Rather I ask you to look at the Jesus of the Bible. Look at him. Don't close your eyes and hope for a word of confirmation. Keep your eyes open and fill them with the full portrait of Jesus provided in the Bible. If you come to trust Jesus Christ as Lord and God, it will be because you see in him a divine glory and excellence that simply is what it is—true.

Sometimes this path is called the "testimony of the Holy Spirit." The old catechisms say it this way: "The Spirit of God, bearing witness by and with the Scriptures in the heart of man, is alone able fully to persuade it that they are the very Word of God."[4] Be sure to notice that the Spirit persuades "by and with the Scriptures." He does not skirt the Scriptures and substitute private revelations about the Scriptures. He removes the blindness of hostility and rebellion, and thus opens the eyes of our hearts to see the self-evident brightness of the divine beauty of Christ.

Therefore, what I have tried to do in this book is to put the biblical portrait of Jesus on display. I have not argued for it historically. Others have done that better than I could, and

I rejoice in their work.[5] I have tried to be faithful to what the Bible really says about Jesus Christ. As imperfect as my writing is, compared to Scripture itself, I still hope that reading these thirteen chapters will be like viewing a diamond through thirteen different facets. The Bible itself is the only authoritative description of the diamond of Jesus Christ. I hope in the end you will turn from this book to the Bible. That is why I have saturated these short chapters with Scripture.

I hope this book will be useful for both believers and unbelievers. I pray that God will use it to awaken unbelievers to see the self-authenticating greatness and glory of Jesus Christ. And I pray that it will sweeten believers' sight of the excellence of Christ.

In this way, the title of the book would come true: *Seeing and Savoring Jesus Christ*. When we see Jesus for who he really is, we savor him. That is, we delight in him as true and beautiful and satisfying. That is my goal, because two things flow from such an experience of Jesus Christ: He is honored, and we are freed by joy to walk the narrow way of love. Christ is most glorified in us when we are most satisfied in him. And when we are satisfied in him, we are crucified to the world. In this way, seeing and savoring Jesus will multiply the mirrors of his presence in the world. As the apostle Paul said, "We all, with unveiled face, *beholding* the glory of the Lord, are *being changed* into his likeness from one degree of glory to another; for this comes from the Lord who is the Spirit" (2 Corinthians 3:18, RSV). Beholding is becoming. Seeing Christ saves and sanctifies.

Since all of this, as Paul says, "comes from . . . the Spirit," I have included prayers after each chapter. The work of the Spirit in our lives is essential. And Jesus said, "If you then, being evil, know how to give good gifts to your children, how much more will your heavenly Father give the Holy Spirit to those who ask Him?" (Luke 11:13). I join with serious readers in asking for greater and fuller measures of the Spirit's work in our lives. As we look to Jesus, may he grant us to see and savor "the glory of God in the face of Christ."

I invite you to join me in this serious quest for well-founded, everlasting, love-producing joy. Everything is at stake. There is no more important issue in life than seeing Jesus for who he really is and savoring what we see above all else.

The heavens are telling

of the glory of God.

PSALM 19:1

✤

God, who said, "Light shall

shine out of darkness," is the One who

has shone in our hearts to give the Light of

the knowledge of the glory of God

in the face of Christ.

2 CORINTHIANS 4:6

✤

1

SEEING AND SAVORING THE GLORY OF GOD

The Ultimate Aim of Jesus Christ

ॐ

The created universe is all about glory. The deepest longing of the human heart and the deepest meaning of heaven and earth are summed up in this: the glory of God. The universe was made to show it, and we were made to see it and savor it. Nothing less will do. Which is why the world is as disordered and as dysfunctional as it is. We have exchanged the glory of God for other things (Romans 1:23).

"The heavens are telling of the glory of God" (Psalm 19:1). That is why all the universe exists. It's all about glory. The Hubble Space Telescope sends back infrared images of faint galaxies perhaps twelve billion light-years away (twelve billion times six trillion miles). Even within our Milky Way there are stars so great as to defy description, like Eta Carinae, which is five million times brighter than our sun.

Sometimes people stumble over this vastness in relation to the apparent insignificance of man. It does seem to make us infinitesimally small. But the meaning of this magnitude is not mainly about us. It's about God. "The heavens are telling of the glory of *God*," says the Scripture. The reason for "wasting" so much space on a universe to house a speck of humanity is to make a point about our Maker, not us. "Lift up your eyes on high and see who has created these stars, the One who leads forth their host by number, He calls them all by name; because of the greatness of His might and the strength of His power, not one of them is missing" (Isaiah 40:26).

The deepest longing of the human heart is to know and enjoy the glory of God. We were made for this. "Bring My sons from afar and My daughters from the ends of the earth . . . whom I have created *for My glory*," says the Lord (Isaiah 43:6-7). To see it, to savor it, and to show it—that is why we exist. The untracked, unimaginable stretches of the created universe are a parable about the inexhaustible "riches of His glory" (Romans 9:23). The physical eye is meant to say to the spiritual eye, "Not this, but the Maker of this, is the Desire of your soul." Saint Paul said, "We exult in hope of the glory of God" (Romans 5:2). Or, even more precisely, he said that we were "prepared beforehand for glory" (Romans 9:23). This is why we were created—that he might "make known the riches of His glory upon vessels of mercy" (Romans 9:23).

The ache in every human heart is an ache for this. But we suppress it and do not see fit to have God in our knowledge (Romans 1:28). Therefore the entire creation has fallen into disorder. The most prominent example of this in the Bible is the disordering of our sexual lives. Paul says that the exchange of the glory of God for other things is the root cause for the homosexual (and heterosexual) disordering of our relationships. "Their women *exchanged* the natural function for that which is unnatural . . . the men abandoned the natural function of the woman and burned in their desire toward one another" (Romans 1:26-27). If we exchange God's glory for lesser things, he gives us up to lived-out parables of depravity—the other exchanges that mirror, in our misery, the ultimate sellout.

The point is this: We were made to know and treasure the glory of God above all things; and when we trade that treasure for images, everything is disordered. The sun of God's glory was made to shine at the center of the solar system of our soul. And when it does, all the planets of our life are held in their proper orbit. But when the sun is displaced, everything flies apart. The healing of the soul begins by restoring the glory of God to its flaming, all-attracting place at the center.

We are all starved for the glory of God, not self. No one goes to the Grand Canyon to increase self-esteem. Why do we go? Because there is greater healing for the soul in beholding splendor than there is in beholding self. Indeed, what could be more ludicrous in a vast and glorious universe like this than a human being, on the speck called earth, standing in front of a mirror trying to find significance in his own self-image? It is a great sadness that this is the gospel of the modern world.

But it is not the Christian Gospel. Into the darkness of petty self-preoccupation has shone "the light of *the gospel of the glory of Christ*, who is the image of God" (2 Corinthians

4:4). The Christian Gospel is about "the glory of Christ," not about me. And when it *is*—in some measure—about me, it is not about my being made much of by God, but about God mercifully enabling me to enjoy making much of him forever.

What was the most loving thing Jesus could do for us? What was the endpoint, the highest good, of the Gospel? Redemption? Forgiveness? Justification? Reconciliation? Sanctification? Adoption? Are not all of these great wonders simply means to something greater? Something final? Something that Jesus asked his Father to give us? "Father, I desire that they also, whom You have given Me, be with Me where I am, *so that they may see My glory* which You have given Me" (John 17:24).

The Christian Gospel is "the gospel of the glory of Christ" because its final aim is that we would see and savor and show the glory of Christ. For this is none other than the glory of God. "He is the radiance of His glory and the exact representation of His nature" (Hebrews 1:3). "He is the image of the invisible God" (Colossians 1:15). When the light of the Gospel shines in our hearts, it is "the Light of the knowledge of the glory of *God* in the face of Christ" (2 Corinthians 4:6). And when we "exult in hope of the glory of God" (Romans 5:2), that hope is "the blessed hope and the appearing of the glory *of our great God* and Savior, Christ Jesus" (Titus 2:13). The glory of Christ is the glory of God. (See Chapter Two.)

In one sense, Christ laid the glory of God aside when he came: "Now, Father, glorify Me together with Yourself, with the glory which *I had* with You before the world was" (John 17:5). But in another sense, Christ manifested the glory of God in his coming: "The Word became flesh, and dwelt among us, and *we saw His glory,* glory as of the only begotten from the Father, full of grace and truth" (John 1:14). Therefore, in the Gospel we see and savor "the glory of God in the face of Christ" (2 Corinthians 4:6). And this kind of "seeing" is the healing of our disordered lives. "We all, with unveiled face, *beholding the glory of the Lord, are being changed* into his likeness from one degree of glory to another" (2 Corinthians 3:18, RSV).

A PRAYER

O Father of glory, this is the cry of our hearts—to be changed from one degree of glory to another, until, in the resurrection, at the last trumpet, we are completely conformed to the image of your Son, Jesus Christ, our Lord. Until then, we long to grow in grace and in the knowledge of our Lord, especially the knowledge of his glory. We want to see it as clearly as we see the sun, and to savor it as deeply as our most desired pleasure. O merciful God, incline our hearts to your Word and the wonders of your glory. Wean us from our obsession with trivial things. Open the eyes of our hearts to see each day what the created universe is telling about your glory. Enlighten our minds to see the glory of your Son in the Gospel. We believe that you are the All-glorious One, and that there is none like you. Help our unbelief. Forgive the wandering of our affections and the undue attention we give to lesser things. Have mercy on us for Christ's sake, and fulfill in us your great design to display the glory of your grace. In Jesus' name we pray, amen.

"Truly, truly, I say to you,

before Abraham was born, I am."

JOHN 8:58

❧

In the beginning was the Word,

and the Word was with God,

and the Word was God.

JOHN 1:1

❧

For in [Christ] all the fullness

of Deity dwells in bodily form.

COLOSSIANS 2:9

❧

2

JESUS IS THE GLORY OF GOD

The Deity of Jesus Christ

※

Christ does not exist in order to make much of us. We exist in order to enjoy making much of him. The assumption of this book is that to know the glories of Christ is an end, not a means. Christ is not glorious so that we get wealthy or healthy. Christ is glorious so that rich or poor, sick or sound, we might be satisfied in him.

The first particular glory that upholds all the rest is the mere eternal existence of Christ. If we will simply ponder this as we ought, a great ballast will come into the tipping ship of our soul. Sheer existence is, perhaps, the greatest mystery of all. Ponder the absoluteness of reality. There had to be something that never came into being. Back, back, back we peer into endless ages, yet there never was nothing. Someone has the honor of being there first and always. He never became or developed. He simply was. To whom belongs this singular, absolute glory?

The answer is Christ, the person whom the world knows as Jesus of Nazareth.

The apostle John, who wrote the last book of the Bible, received the decisive revelation. He quotes God: "'I am the Alpha and the Omega,' says the Lord God, 'who is and who was and who is to come, the Almighty'" (Revelation 1:8). This is not Christ talking. This is the Almighty God. He calls himself "Alpha and Omega"—the first and last letters of the Greek alphabet. In the alphabet, one cannot speak of anything (or nothing) before alpha. There is no "before" alpha in the alphabet. Nor can one speak of anything (or nothing) after omega. There is no "after" omega in the alphabet.

So it is with God and reality. There is no "before" God and no "after" God. He is absolutely there, no matter how far back or how far forward you go. He is the absolute Reality. He has the honor of being there first and always. To him belongs this singular glory.

This is the essential meaning of his Old Testament name Yahweh (or Jehovah). It is built on the verb "to be." When Moses asked God his name, "God said to Moses, '*I AM WHO I AM* . . . you shall say to the sons of Israel, '*I AM* has sent me to you'" (Exodus 3:14). This "I am" is unfolded by God in Isaiah as implying absolute, eternal Reality—past and future. "'You are My witnesses,' declares the LORD . . . 'so that you may know and believe Me and understand that *I am* He. *Before* Me there was no God formed, and there will be none *after* Me'" (Isaiah 43:10). To be "I am" is to be absolutely the first and the last. No "before" and no "after." Simply "I am."

God makes this explicit in Isaiah 44:6, "Thus says the LORD, the King of Israel and his Redeemer, the LORD of hosts:

'I am *the first* and I am *the last*, and there is no God besides Me.'" And again in Isaiah 48:12, "Listen to Me, O Jacob, even Israel whom I called; I am He, I am *the first*, I am also *the last*." This is his name: *Yahweh*—the one who absolutely, eternally, and invincibly is. He has the unique honor and singular glory of *always having been*, when nothing else was. Nor will he be outlasted by anything. This is what it means to be God.

What, then, does this have to do with Christ, whom we know as Jesus of Nazareth?

Everything. The apostle John quoted Christ near the end of his Revelation: "Behold, I am coming quickly. . . . *I am the Alpha and the Omega, the first and the last, the beginning and the end*. . . . I, Jesus, have sent My angel to testify to you these things for the churches" (Revelation 22:12-13, 16). This is Christ talking, not God the Father. Now, two cannot be "Alpha and Omega" unless they are one. Two cannot be absolutely "first and last" unless they are one. Yet Christ (who calls himself Jesus) claims for himself the same honor and glory belonging to God the Almighty (see also Revelation 1:17-18; 2:8).

Christ even took to himself the uniquely glorious name of God, "I am." "Jesus said to them, 'Truly, truly, I say to you, before Abraham was born, *I am*'" (John 8:58). "From now on," Jesus says to his disciples near the end of his life, "I am telling you before it comes to pass, so that when it does occur, you may believe that *I am*" (John 13:19, author's translation; see John 8:24). Nothing greater can any man say of himself. It is true, or it is blasphemy. Christ was God or godless.

John knew which. "In the beginning was the Word, and

the Word was with God, and *the Word was God*. . . . And the Word became flesh . . . the only begotten from the Father" (John 1:1, 14). Jesus Christ, the "Word," was "begotten," not made—and not at any point in time, but eternally. Two Persons standing forth as one God, not two Gods—the "Son" begotten from the "Father," one essential deity. This is a great mystery, as we would expect it to be. But it is what God has revealed about himself.

The apostle Paul also knew the unique glory that belonged to Christ. He is "the Christ according to the flesh, who is over all, *God* blessed forever. Amen" (Romans 9:5). Nevertheless, "although He existed *in the form of God*, [He] did not regard *equality with God* a thing to be grasped, but emptied Himself, taking the form of a bond-servant" (Philippians 2:6-7). Therefore, "in him *the whole fullness of deity* dwells bodily" (Colossians 2:9, RSV; see 1:19). And we Christians are now waiting not for a mere man, but for "the appearing of the glory of our great *God* and Savior, *Christ Jesus*" (Titus 2:13; see also 2 Peter 1:1).

This is why the writer to the Hebrews is so bold as to say all the angels *worship* Christ. He is not the chief among angels who worship God. He is *worshiped* by all angels *as* God. "And when [God] again brings the firstborn into the world, He says, 'Let all the angels of God worship Him'" (Hebrews 1:6). For he is the Creator of all that is, and is himself God: "Of the Son [God] says, 'Your throne, *O God*, is forever and ever. . . . You, Lord, in the beginning laid the foundation of the earth'" (Hebrews 1:8, 10). Thus the Father bears witness to the deity of the Son. He "is the radiance of His glory and the exact representation of His nature, and upholds all things by the word of His power" (Hebrews 1:3).

Jesus Christ is the Creator of the universe. Jesus Christ is the Alpha and Omega, the first and the last. Jesus Christ, the Person, never had a beginning. He is absolute Reality. He has the unparalleled honor and unique glory of being there first and always. He never came into being. He was eternally begotten. The Father has eternally enjoyed "the radiance of His glory and the exact representation of His nature" (Hebrews 1:3) in the Person of his Son.

Seeing and savoring this glory is the goal of our salvation. "Father, I desire that they also, whom You have given Me, be with Me where I am, so *that they may see My glory* which You have given Me" (John 17:24). To feast on this forever is the aim of our being created and our being redeemed.

A PRAYER

Eternal Father, you never had a beginning. You will never have an ending. You are the Alpha and the Omega. This we believe, because you have revealed it to us. Our hearts leap up with gratitude that you have opened our eyes to see and know that Jesus Christ is your eternal, divine Son, begotten, not made, and that you, O Father, and he, your Son, are one God. We tremble even to take such glorious truths on our lips for fear of dishonoring you with withering and inadequate words. But we must speak, because we must praise you. Silence would shame us, and the rocks themselves would cry out. You must be praised for who you are in the world you have made. And we must thank you because you have made us taste and see the glory of Jesus Christ, your Son. Oh, to know him! Father, we long to know him. Banish from our minds low thoughts of Christ. Saturate our souls with the Spirit of Christ and all his greatness. Enlarge our capacities to be satisfied in all that you are for us in him. Where flesh and blood are impotent, reveal to us the Christ, and rivet our attention and our affections on the truth and beauty of your all-glorious Son. And grant that whether rich or poor, sick or sound, we might be transformed by him and become an echo of his excellence in the world. In Jesus' name we pray, amen.

I saw . . . a Lamb standing,

as if slain,

having seven horns

and seven eyes.

REVELATION 5:6

3

THE LION AND THE LAMB

The Excellence of Jesus Christ

❧

A lion is admirable for its ferocious strength and imperial appearance. A lamb is admirable for its meekness and servant-like provision of wool for our clothing. But even more admirable is a lion-like lamb and a lamb-like lion. What makes Christ glorious, as Jonathan Edwards observed over 250 years ago, is "an admirable conjunction of diverse excellencies."[1]

For example, we admire Christ for his transcendence, but even more because the transcendence of his greatness is mixed with submission to God. We marvel at him because his uncompromising justice is tempered with mercy. His majesty is sweetened by meekness. In his equality *with* God he has a deep reverence *for* God. Though he is worthy of all good, he was patient to suffer evil. His sovereign dominion over the world was clothed with a spirit of obedience and submission. He baffled the proud scribes with his wisdom, but was simple enough to be loved by children. He could still the storm with a word, but would not strike the Samaritans with lightning or take himself down from the cross.

The glory of Christ is not a simple thing. It is a coming together in one person of extremely diverse qualities. We see it in the New Testament book of Revelation: "The *Lion* that is from the tribe of Judah, the Root of David, has overcome so as to open the book and its seven seals" (5:5). Here is the triumphant lion-like Christ ready to unroll the scroll of history.

But what do we see in the next verse? "I saw between the throne (with the four living creatures) and the elders a *Lamb* standing, as if slain, having seven horns and seven eyes, which are the seven Spirits of God, sent out into all the earth" (verse 6). So the Lion is a Lamb—an animal that is weak and harmless and lowly and easily preyed upon, and sheared naked for clothes, and killed for our food. So Christ is a lamb-like Lion.

The Lion of Judah conquered because he was willing to act the part of a lamb. He came into Jerusalem on Palm Sunday like a king on the way to a throne, and he went out of Jerusalem on Good Friday like a lamb on the way to the slaughter. He drove out the robbers from the Temple like a lion devouring its prey. And then at the end of the week he gave his majestic neck to the knife, and they slaughtered the Lion of Judah like a sacrificial lamb.

But what sort of lamb? Revelation 5:6 says, the "Lamb [was] standing, as if slain, having seven horns." Notice two things. First, the Lamb is "standing." It is not slumped in a bloody heap on the ground as it once was. Yes, it had been slain. But now it is standing—standing in the innermost circle next to the throne.

Second, the Lamb has seven horns. A horn is a symbol of strength and power throughout the book of Revelation (12:3; 13:1; 17:3, 12), as well as in the Old Testament (Deuteronomy 33:17; Psalm 18:2; 112:9). And the number seven signifies fullness and completeness. So this is no ordinary lamb. He is alive from the dead, and he is completely mighty in his sevenfold strength. He is, in fact, a lion-like Lamb.

We see this with trembling in Revelation 6:16, where men call to the mountains and rocks, "Fall on us and hide us from . . . the wrath of the Lamb." And we see it in Revelation 17:14, "These will wage war against the Lamb, and the Lamb will overcome them, because He is Lord of lords and King of kings."

So Christ is a lamb-like Lion and a lion-like Lamb. That is his glory—"an admirable conjunction of diverse excellencies."

This glorious conjunction shines all the brighter because it corresponds perfectly with our personal weariness and our longing for greatness. Jesus said, "Come to Me, all who are weary and heavy-laden, and I will give you rest. Take My yoke upon you and learn from Me, for I am gentle and humble in heart" (Matthew 11:28-29). The lamb-like gentleness and humility of this Lion woos us in our weariness. And we love him for it. If he only recruited like the Marines, who want strength, we would despair of coming.

But this quality of meekness alone would not be glorious. The gentleness and humility of the lamb-like Lion become brilliant alongside the limitless and everlasting authority of the lion-like Lamb. Only this fits our longing for greatness. Yes, we are weak and weary and heavy-laden. But there burns in every heart, at least from time to time, a dream that our lives will count for something great. To this dream Jesus said, "All authority has been given to Me in heaven and on earth. Go therefore and make disciples of all the nations . . . and lo, I am with you always, even to the end of the age" (Matthew 28:18-20).

The lion-like Lamb calls us to take heart from his absolute authority over all reality. And he reminds us that, in all that authority, he will be with us to the end of the age. This is what we long for—a champion, an invincible leader. We mere mortals are not simple either. We are pitiful, yet we have mighty passions. We are weak, yet we dream of doing wonders. We are transient, but eternity is written on our hearts. The glory of Christ shines all the brighter because the conjunction of his diverse excellencies corresponds perfectly to our complexity.

Once, this lamb-like Lion was oppressed and afflicted. He was led to the slaughter. Like a sheep that is silent before its shearers, he did not open his mouth (Isaiah 53:7). But at the last day it will not be so. The lamb-like Lion will become a lion-like Lamb, and with imperial aplomb he will take his stand on the shore of the lake of fire, where his impenitent enemies will "be tormented . . . in the presence of the holy angels and in the presence of the Lamb . . . forever and ever" (Revelation 14:10-11).

A PRAYER

Almighty and merciful God, we exult in the reflection of your might and mercy in your Son, our Lord, Jesus Christ. We rejoice in the strength of his lion-like power and in the tenderness of his lamb-like meekness. We take heart from his incomparable combination of excellencies. It reassures us that there is none like him, and that he is not a mere man like others. O grant us, in our brash indifference, to tremble before the Lion of Judah and to humble ourselves under his fierce holiness. And grant us, in our brokenness and fear, to gather courage from the lion-like Lamb. Oh, how we need the whole Christ! Open our eyes to see the fullness of his excellence. Remove the lopsided and distorted images of your Son that weaken our worship and lame our obedience. May the power of the Lion and the love of the Lamb make our faith in Christ unshakable. So deliver us from small dreams and timid ventures and halting plans. Embolden us. Strengthen us. Make us love with fierce and humble love. Let us share the confidence of the Lion of Judah that gave him the will to die like a Lamb and rise in everlasting joy. And in it all, grant that all might see the glory of Christ and that you might be honored through him. In Jesus' name we pray, amen.

"God, Your God,

has anointed you with

the oil of gladness

above your companions."

HEBREWS 1:9

✤

"Well done, good and faithful servant. . . .

Enter into the joy of your master."

MATTHEW 25:21, RSV

✤

4

The Indestructible Joy

The Gladness of Jesus Christ

❧

If a lifeguard saves you from the undertow of the Atlantic Ocean, you don't care if he is gloomy. It doesn't matter what his mental state is when you are hugging your family on the beach. But with the salvation of Jesus, things are very different. Jesus does not save us for our family, but for himself. If he is gloomy, our salvation will be sad. And that is no great salvation.

Jesus *himself*—and all that God is for us in him—is our great reward, nothing less. "I am the bread of life. . . . If anyone is thirsty, let him come to Me" (John 6:35; 7:37). Salvation is not mainly the forgiveness of sins, but mainly the fellowship of Jesus (1 Corinthians 1:9). Forgiveness gets everything out of the way so this can happen. If this fellowship is not all-satisfying, there is no great salvation. If Christ is gloomy, or even calmly stoical, eternity will be a long, long sigh.

But the *glory* and *grace* of Jesus is that he is, and always will be, indestructibly happy. I say it is his *glory*, because gloom is not glorious. And I say it is his *grace*, because the best thing he has to give us is his joy. "These things I have spoken to you, that *my joy* may be in you, and that your joy may be full" (John 15:11, RSV; see also 17:13). It would not be fully gracious of Jesus simply to increase *my* joy to its final limit and then leave me short of his. My capacities for joy are very confined. So Christ not only offers himself as the divine object of my joy, but pours his capacity for joy into me, so that I can enjoy him with the very joy of God. This is glory, and this is grace.

It is not glorious to be gloomy. Therefore Christ has never been gloomy. From eternity he has been the mirror of God's infinite mirth. The Wisdom of God spoke these words in Proverbs 8:30, "Then I was beside Him, as a master workman; and I was daily His delight, rejoicing always before Him." The eternal Christ, God's happy and equal agent in creation, was ever rejoicing before God and ever God's delight. Twice more we see this in the New Testament.

In Hebrews 1:8-9 God speaks to the Son, not to the angels, with these astonishing words: "Your throne, O God, is forever and ever. . . . You have loved righteousness and hated lawlessness; therefore God, Your God, has anointed you with the oil of *gladness* above your companions." Jesus Christ is the happiest being in the universe. His gladness is greater than all the angelic gladness of heaven. He mirrors perfectly the infinite, holy, indomitable mirth of his Father.

Again, in Acts 2:25-31 Peter interprets Psalm 16 to refer to Christ: "I saw the Lord always before Me; for He is at My right hand that I may not be shaken. Therefore My heart was *glad*, and My tongue *rejoiced.* . . . For You will not abandon my soul to Hades, nor let your Holy One see corruption. . . . You will make Me full of *gladness* with Your presence" (author's translation). The risen Christ will shake off the shades of death and be glad with the very gladness of God. The glory of Christ is his infinite, eternal, indestructible gladness in the presence of God.

But if it is not glorious to be gloomy, neither is it glorious to be glib. The carefree merriment of a ballroom gala and the irrepressible joy in a Russian gulag are not the same. One is trite, the other triumphant. One is glib, the other glorious. There is a pasted smile that has never known pain. And it does not make for a good pastor or a great Savior. But Christ *is* a great Savior.

Therefore, this man of indestructible joy was "a man of sorrows and acquainted with grief" (Isaiah 53:3). "My soul is very sorrowful, even to death; remain here, and watch with me" (Matthew 26:38, RSV). This "great High Priest" is not unable to sympathize with us in our weaknesses, because he was tested in every way as a man like us (Hebrews 4:14-15). He wept with those who wept (John 11:35) and rejoiced with those who rejoiced (Luke 10:17, 21). He was hungry (Matthew 4:2), he was weary (John 4:6), he was forsaken (Matthew 26:56), and betrayed (Matthew 26:45), whipped (Matthew 27:26), mocked (Matthew 27:31), and crucified (Matthew 27:35).

Indomitable joy does not mean that there is only joy. Was he then divided, torn between joy and sorrow? Can an infinitely glorious soul be troubled? Yes, troubled, but not torn and disunited. Christ was complex, but he was not confused. There were divergent notes in the music of his soul, but the result was a symphony. A general's complex battle strategy may suffer the enemy to have temporary and apparent tactical triumphs, only to gain a greater victory in the end. This is not a mark of confusion in the mind of the general. It may appear so to those who see only part of the field. But it is his glory. The Pacific Ocean may have a thousand squalls, but from a hundred miles in the air it is one great, deep, calm, and glorious mass of replenishing water.

Through the agonies of Gethsemane and Golgotha, Jesus was sustained by indestructible joy. "For the *joy* that was set before him [he] endured the cross, despising the shame, and is seated at the right hand of the throne of God" (Hebrews 12:2, RSV). And what was that all-sustaining gladness? It was the gladness of receiving worship from those he died to make glad in God. The Good Shepherd rejoices over one lost sheep (Matthew 18:13). How much more over countless armies of the ransomed!

Is there a lesson here for how we should suffer? Have you ever noticed that we are not only to imitate the Lord's *suffering*, but the Lord's *joy* in it? Paul said to the Thessalonians, "You became imitators . . . of the Lord, for you received the word in much affliction with the *joy* of the Holy Spirit" (1 Thessalonians 1:6, author's translation). It was the joy of the Lord in affliction that filled this young church.

This is a call to us now in our day. Will we embrace suffering for the cause of Christ? Not joylessness, but suffering.

Will we heed the call in Hebrews 13:13 (RSV), "Let us go forth
to him outside the camp and bear the abuse he endured"? The
answer is going to hang on whether the city of God is more
desirable to us than the city of man. Will we answer, "Here we
have no lasting city, but we seek the city which is to come"
(Hebrews 13:14, RSV)? Or will we cling to the fleeting pleasures
of Egypt (Hebrews 11:25-26)?

For those who have tasted the joy of Jesus, surely nothing
is more compelling than the all-surpassing hope of hearing
his final word, "Well done, good and faithful servant. . . . Enter
into the *joy* of your master" (Matthew 25:21, RSV). The city
of God is a city of joy. And that joy is the indestructible joy
of Christ.

A P R A Y E R

Father, it is a great comfort to us that you and your
Son are never glib and never gloomy. We delight in
the truth that you can be infinitely happy without
being callous to our pain. We stand in wonder that the
light of Jesus' joy makes a rainbow in the tears on his
face. We long to be like this. We want to be strong
and unshakable in the joy of our faith. But we don't
want to be oblivious to the grievousness of our own
sin or the pain of other people's distress. O God, ful-
fill in us the purpose of your Son in promising that
his joy would be in us and that our joy would be full.

Make the fruit of the Spirit—joy—flourish in our lives. Satisfy us in the morning with your steadfast love that we may rejoice and be glad in you. Waken our slumbering souls from the sleep of listlessness. Take away the lukewarmness of our hearts. Fan the flame of zeal for the glory of your name. May Christ so dwell in our hearts with his indestructible joy that day by day we are conformed more and more to his glad image. And so may we be a place of refuge and eternal refreshment for a hopeless, joy-seeking world of people who do not know they are starved for the glory of the gladness of God in Jesus Christ. In his name we pray, amen.

There's not a plant or flower below,

But makes Thy glories known;

And clouds arise, and tempests blow,

By order from Thy throne.

ISAAC WATTS
"I Sing the Mighty Power of God"

❧

"Who then is this,

that even the wind

and the sea obey Him?"

MARK 4:41

❧

5

The Waves and Winds
Still Know His Voice

The Power of Jesus Christ

✤

In July 1995, my wife, Noël, two of our children, and I huddled on the floor, away from all windows, under the direct path of Hurricane Erin in Pensacola, Florida. One magnificent old pine tree sheared off the corner of our bedroom as it fell. During the eye of the storm we walked outside in a perfect calm to see the devastation. Then, about twenty minutes later, we hid again against the backside of the storm as it brought down chimneys and crushed cars under snapped-off oak limbs as thick as hundred-year-old trees.

God strolled the beach—
Our legs and faces could not bear the piercing, blasting sand.

God stepped ashore—
Palms waved, scattering branches in his path.

God strode inland—
Magnolias, pines, and oaks,
Who'd stretched one hundred years toward God,
Fell to the ground before him.

God stood and breathed—
While we—in dark, closed closet—
Feared to face his glory.

It was a heart-wrenching, worship-filled moment in the face of raw, unstoppable power. The losses were painful, though nothing like the destruction of Hurricane Mitch in Honduras in 1998, which took 10,000 lives—and which in turn was small compared to the cyclone that killed 131,000 in Bangladesh on April 30, 1991, and left nine million homeless. Beneath the wreckage of such wind you have two choices: worship or curse.

It was wind that killed Job's ten children. "A great wind came from across the wilderness and struck the four corners of the house, and it fell on the young people and they died" (Job 1:19). When boils were added to that, Job's wife said, "*Curse* God and die" (Job 2:9). But Job's response to the death of his children was different: "Job arose and tore his robe and shaved his head, and he fell to the ground and *worshiped*. He said . . . 'The LORD gave and the LORD has taken away. Blessed be the name of the LORD'" (Job 1:20-21). And when the boils were added to his grief, he said to his wife: "Shall we indeed receive good from God and not receive adversity?" (Job 2:10, author's translation).

Both, not just the one, are the work of God and the ground of worship. Later in Job, Elihu says it clearly: "Out of the south comes the storm. . . . [God] disperses the cloud of His lightning. It changes direction, turning around by His guidance, that it may do whatever He commands it on the face of the inhabited earth. Whether for correction . . . or for lovingkindness, He causes it to happen. . . . Stand and consider the wonders of God" (Job 37:9-14).

Psalm 29 considers and celebrates this one wonder: the thunderstorm. "The God of glory thunders. . . . The voice of the LORD is full of majesty. The voice of the LORD breaks the cedars. . . . The voice of the LORD . . . strips the forests bare; and in his temple all cry, 'Glory!'" (Psalm 29:3-5, 9-10, author's translation).

It is the glory of God to bare his mighty arm in wind and thunder. "The LORD is great. . . . Whatever the LORD pleases, He does, in heaven and in earth. . . . [He] makes lightnings for the rain, [and] brings forth the wind from His treasuries" (Psalm 135:5-7). "Praise the LORD from the earth, sea monsters and all deeps; fire and hail, snow and clouds; stormy wind, fulfilling His word" (Psalm 148:7-8). Isaac Watts had his feet on the earth and his head in heaven when he wrote, "Clouds arise, and tempests blow, by order from Thy throne."

Therefore it is not surprising that when Christ came into the world, all nature bowed to his authority. He commanded the wind and it obeyed. And when the disciples saw it they wondered. And then worshiped. "There arose a fierce gale of wind, and the waves were breaking over the boat. . . . And

[Jesus] got up and rebuked the wind and said to the sea, 'Hush, be still.' And the wind died down and it became perfectly calm. . . . [The disciples] became very much afraid and said to one another, 'Who then is this, that even the wind and the sea obey Him?'" (Mark 4:37-41).

Water obeyed Jesus in more ways than one. When he commanded, it became "solid" under his feet, and he walked on it. When the disciples saw this they "worshiped him saying, 'Truly you are the Son of God'" (Matthew 14:33, RSV). Another time, he commanded water, and it became wine at the wedding of Cana. In response, John says, he "manifested His glory, and His disciples believed in Him" (John 2:11). Wind and water do whatever the Lord Jesus tells them to do. Be still. Bear weight. Become wine. Natural laws were made by Christ and alter at his bidding.

The composition of all things was not only created by Christ (John 1:3; Colossians 1:16; Hebrews 1:2), but is also held in being moment by moment throughout the whole universe by his will. "He . . . upholds all things by the word of His power" (Hebrews 1:3). "In Him all things hold together" (Colossians 1:17). Jesus Christ defines reality in the beginning and gives it form every second.

Fatalities, fevers, fish, food, fig trees. Anywhere you turn, Christ is the absolute master over all material substance. With a word he commands the dead to live again. "Lazarus, come forth!" (John 11:43). "Young man, arise!" (Luke 7:14). "'Talitha kum!' (which means, 'Little girl . . . get up!')" (Mark 5:41). He rebuked a fever and it left Peter's mother-in-law

(Luke 4:39). He planned for a fish to swallow a coin and then get caught with Peter's hook (Matthew 17:27). He took five loaves and fed five thousand men (Matthew 14:19-21). And he made a fig tree wither with his curse (Mark 11:21).

Now we have a choice. Worship or curse. There was a group at Lazarus' grave whose facts were right and hearts were wrong. They said, "Could not he who opened the eyes of the blind man have kept this man from dying?" (John 11:37, RSV). The answer to that question is, Yes. Jesus timed his coming to Lazarus' home so as to let his friend die. He waited two days, then said, "Lazarus is dead, and I am glad for your sakes that I was not there, so that you may believe" (John 11:14-15). Yes, he could have saved him. Just as he could have saved Job's children, and ten thousand more in Honduras and Guatemala by commanding Hurricane Mitch to turn out to sea, the way he did in Galilee.

Will we worship or will we curse the One who rules the world? Shall sinners dictate who should live and who should die? Or shall we say with Hannah, "The LORD brings death and makes alive; he brings down to the grave and raises up" (1 Samuel 2:6, NIV)? And shall we, with ashes on our heads, worship with Job, "Blessed be the name of the LORD" (Job 1:21)? Will we learn from James that there is good purpose in it all: "You have heard of the steadfastness of Job, and you have seen the *purpose* of the Lord, how the Lord is compassionate and merciful" (James 5:11, RSV)? Should we not then face the wind and stand on the waves of affliction and sing with Katharina von Schlegel,

Be still, my soul! Your God will undertake
To guide the future as He has the past;
Your hope, your confidence let nothing shake;
All now mysterious shall be bright at last.
Be still, my soul! The waves and winds still know
His voice who ruled them while He dwelt below.
"BE STILL MY SOUL"

A PRAYER

O Lord, the suffering in the world is so widespread and the pain is so great! Have mercy, and waken the souls of suffering millions to the hope of some relief now and unsurpassed joy in the age to come. Send your church, O God, with relief and with the word of the Gospel that there is forgiveness of sins through faith in Christ and that no suffering here is worth comparing to the glory that will be revealed to the children of God. Protect your church, Father, from callous thoughts about calamities that leave millions destitute, and protect her also from cowing to critics, like Job's wife, who cannot trust the wisdom and power and goodness of Christ in the midst of inexplicable misery. Oh, help our unbelief. Incline our hearts to your Word and to its assurances that you "work all things according to the counsel of your will" and that "no purpose of yours can be thwarted" and that you are doing good and acting wisely in ways that we cannot now even dream. Keep us in peace, O Lord, and forbid that we murmur and complain. Grant us humble and submissive hearts under your mighty hand. Teach us to wait and watch for your final and holy purposes in all things. Grant that we would "rejoice in hope" even when present circumstances bring us to tears. Open the eyes of our hearts to see the greatness of our inheritance in Christ, and send us with tender hands to touch with mercy the miseries of the world. In Jesus' name we pray, amen.

"Lord, You know all things."

JOHN 21:17

✤

"I am telling you before it comes to pass,

so that when it does occur,

you may believe that I am."

JOHN 13:19,
AUTHOR'S TRANSLATION

✤

6

SOMETHING GREATER THAN SOLOMON IS HERE

The Wisdom of Jesus Christ

※

Many who have set out to silence Jesus have said in the end, "No man ever spoke like this man" (John 7:46, RSV). One reason is the incomparable wisdom and knowledge of Jesus.

The Queen of Sheba was so stunned at the wisdom and knowledge of Solomon that when she had seen all his house and heard his answers to her questions, "there was no more spirit in her" (1 Kings 10:5). It took her breath away. What then does it mean when Jesus says, "The Queen of the South will rise up with this generation at the judgment and will condemn it, because she came from the ends of the earth to hear the wisdom of Solomon; and behold, something greater than Solomon is here" (Matthew 12:42)?

Not even the wisest of all kings spoke like this man. Someone had come onto the scene of history unparalleled in knowledge and wisdom. Up to a point Jesus was willing to dialogue with the wise men of his day. But when the hour came, and he was ready, he spoke the decisive sentence that ended the conversation ("If David then calls Him 'Lord,' how is He his son?" [Matthew 22:45]). And "no one was able to answer Him a word, nor did anyone dare from that day on to ask Him another question" (Matthew 22:46). His knowledge and wisdom made him master of every situation. One reason to admire and trust Jesus above all other persons is that his knowledge and wisdom are unsurpassed.

He knows all people thoroughly, our hearts and our thoughts. John paid tribute to this vast knowledge when he said that Jesus did not entrust himself to men because "He knew all men, and because He did not need anyone to testify concerning man, for He Himself knew what was in man" (John 2:24-25). He knows all our thoughts before we express them. He sees where no one else can see. Nothing is hidden from his eyes. "And Jesus knowing their thoughts said, 'Why are you thinking evil in your hearts?'" (Matthew 9:4). Thus it was the confession of the early church: "You, Lord . . . know the hearts of all men" (Acts 1:24).

There is no one who perplexes Jesus. No thought or action is unintelligible to him. He knows its origin and end. The most convoluted psychotic and the most abstruse genius are open and laid bare to his understanding. He understands every motion of every mind.

Jesus not only knows all of us as we are today, he also knows what we will think and do tomorrow. He knows all things that will come to pass. John's Gospel stresses this, because John sees it as part of Jesus' divine majesty. "Jesus [knew] all the things that were coming upon Him" (John 18:4). On the basis of this knowledge he foretold numerous things that his friends and enemies would do. "Jesus knew from the beginning who they were who did not believe, and who it was that would betray Him" (John 6:64). "From now on," he said, "I am telling you before it comes to pass, so that when it does occur, you may believe that I am" (John 13:19, author's translation).

In other words, the reason he foretold these things is so that we might believe that "he is." Is what? That he is the divine Son of God. "I AM" is the name for God in Exodus 3:14 and the designation of deity in Isaiah 43:10. This, very likely, is the way Jesus understood it when he used the words absolutely: "Truly, truly, I say to you, before Abraham was born, I am" (John 8:58). Jesus wants us to believe that he is God. That is why he says, "Behold, I have told you in advance" (Matthew 24:25). His foreknowledge is essential to his divinity.

The extent of Jesus' knowledge is a compelling warrant for faith in his divine origin. Thus his disciples said, "Now we know that You know all things, and have no need for anyone to question You; by this we believe that You came from God" (John 16:30). At the end of his time on earth, Jesus queried Peter three times, "'Simon, son of John, do you love Me?' Peter was grieved because He said to him the third time, 'Do you love Me?' And he said to Him, 'Lord, You know all things; You know that I love You'" (John 21:17). Peter did not conclude from Jesus' knowledge of his heart that he knew all things; rather he concluded from the omniscience of Jesus that he knew his heart. "You know all things" is a general and unqualified statement of John's Gospel—Jesus knows all that is and all that shall come to pass.

The closest thing to a contradiction of this claim is Matthew 24:36 where Jesus says, concerning the Second Coming, "Of that day and hour no one knows, not even the angels of heaven, nor the Son, but the Father alone." I take this to mean that in his human nature, but not his divine nature, Jesus did not know the time of his Second Coming. How the two natures of Christ cohere as human and divine in one Person is one of the greatest mysteries of the universe.[1]

The greatest thing that can be said of Jesus' knowledge is that he knows God perfectly. He knows God perfectly, because he is God. We know God partially and imperfectly. Jesus knows him like no other being knows him. He knows him the way an omniscient person knows himself. "All things have been handed over to Me by My Father; and no one knows the Son except the Father; nor does anyone know the Father except the Son, and anyone to whom the Son wills to reveal Him" (Matthew 11:27). No one but Jesus knows the Father immediately, completely, and perfectly. Our knowledge of the Father depends wholly on Jesus' gracious revelation; our knowledge is derivative and partial and, because of our sin, imperfect.

Nothing greater can be said about the knowledge of Jesus than that he knows God perfectly. All reality outside God is parochial compared to the infinite reality that God is. What God has made is like a toy compared to the complexity and depth of who God is. All the sciences that scratch the surface of the created universe are mere ABCs compared to Christ's exhaustive knowledge of the created universe. And even this knowledge of the created universe is a dewdrop on a blade of grass compared to the ocean of knowledge that Jesus has of the being of God himself. While the universe is finite, God is infinite. Complete knowledge of the infinite is infinite. Therefore to know God as Jesus knows God is to have infinite knowledge.

Therefore, let us bow down and worship Jesus Christ. Even if we are impressed with the scholarship of man and the achievements of scientific knowledge, let us not play the fool by trumpeting the wonder of these tiny chirps while ignoring the thunderclap of Christ's omniscience. Jesus alone is worthy of our highest admiration. Jesus alone is worthy of our trust. He can show us the Father (Matthew 11:27). He can give us irresistible wisdom (Luke 21:15). He can see how to make all things work together for our good (Romans 8:28). Not one of his judgments about anything is ever mistaken (John 8:16). He teaches the way of God with infallible truthfulness (Matthew 22:16). Trust him. Admire him. Follow him. For "in [him] are hidden all the treasures of wisdom and knowledge" (Colossians 2:3).

A   P R A Y E R

Father, we say with the psalmist, such knowledge is too wonderful for us, it is too high, we cannot attain it. We stand in awe of your infinite knowledge and wisdom. We are filled with questions. But you are filled with answers. There is no mystery to you. There are no facts you do not know, no problems you cannot solve, no events you cannot explain, no hypocrisy through which you do not see. Oh, grant us to see and feel that your all-knowing mind, together with your power and grace, makes you utterly trustworthy. Your counsel takes everything into account, including the past and the future. Your good plan will never be altered owing to unforeseen events. We can count on you. And as we do, Father, share with us, we pray, enough of your great wisdom and enough of your great knowledge that we may live and love and, finally, die in a way that brings life to others, satisfies our soul, and honors you. The lips of the wise are a fountain of life, and oh, how we long to bring life to the perishing. Grant us your wisdom in the measure we can bear. In Jesus' name, amen.

A good name is to be chosen

rather than great riches.

PROVERBS 22:1, RSV

❧

"'Behold, a glutton and a drunkard,

a friend of tax collectors

and sinners!'"

MATTHEW 11:19, RSV

❧

7

THE GLORIOUS POVERTY OF A BAD REPUTATION

The Desecration of Jesus Christ

⚘

If "a good name is to be chosen rather than great riches" (Proverbs 22:1, RSV), Jesus was doubly poor. Not only did he "empty himself" of the glorious riches of heaven (Philippians 2:7-8) in order to live among us as one who had "nowhere to lay His head" (Luke 9:58), but through it all, his reputation was stained again and again. The slander was unrelenting. The rumors were incorrigible. The half-truths were too devious to answer. And in the end, the "good name" of the greatest man was ruined in Jerusalem. The crowds that had hailed him as king crucified him as criminal.

But oh, what splendor lies hidden behind every one of those scandals! Consider the honors of our King in all the calumny he endured.

It began with his birth. The scandal was inevitable, and God knew it. Jesus' mother was pregnant before she was married. Joseph was not the father. So Matthew says, "Being a righteous man and not wanting to disgrace her, Joseph planned to send her away secretly" (Matthew 1:19). That was not God's plan. Eliminating disgrace was not his agenda.

We do not know what Mary suffered. But we get a glimpse of what Jesus endured. His enemies always had this trump card they could throw on the table when the force of truth turned against them. In John 8, Jesus was uncovering their deep duplicity and slavery to sin, even implying that the devil was their father. When Jesus said, "You are doing the deeds of your father," they reached for the card and said, "*We* were not born of fornication; we have one Father: God" (verse 41). The indictment was not veiled: they were calling Jesus a bastard. Even into the third century, Origen was still answering this slander in the writings of Celsus.

But what an honor lay hidden behind this insult! Yes, Mary was pregnant before she was married. Yes, Joseph was not the father. But no, Jesus was not illegitimate. There is another reality: "The angel . . . said to [Mary], 'The Holy Spirit will come upon you, and the power of the Most High will overshadow you; and for that reason the holy Child shall be called the Son of God'" (Luke 1:35). There was no other birth like this one. For there is only one Son of God. One spotless human. One God-Man. One perfect Lamb to take away the sin of the world. Oh, what beautiful truths lay hidden beneath the lies of Jesus' foes.

When someone hates your cause, all strategies of love will be slandered, even opposite ones. Jesus was astonished at this in his generation: "To what shall I compare this generation? It is like children sitting in the market places" (Matthew 11:16). They won't dance with the flute and they won't weep with the dirge. For them the music of truth is never right. John the Baptist was the dirge. Jesus was the flute. And his generation would hear neither. How shall these two be silenced? Slander.

"For John came neither eating nor drinking, and they say, 'He has a demon!' The Son of man came eating and drinking, and they say, 'Behold, a gluttonous man and a drunkard, a friend of tax collectors and sinners!'" (Matthew 11:18-19). Truth came dressed in camel skins and eating locusts and living in the wilderness and calling kings adulterers and doing no miracles and dying for a dancing girl. And this was not acceptable. So truth came sociably and went to feasts and made fine wine and let a harlot wash its feet. But this too was not acceptable.

What this meant was that form was not the stumbling block. Truth itself was the stumbling block. And so the only escape for the enemies of truth was caricature and half-truth. Jesus is a glutton and drunkard. That is why he eats with tax collectors and sinners. But beneath the ugliness of calumny is the glory of compassion. Why did he eat with tax collectors and sinners? He gave the answer himself: "Those who are well have no need of a physician, but those who are sick; I have not come to call the righteous, but sinners to repentance" (Luke 5:31-32, RSV). Behind the slander of gluttony is the splendor of mercy. Jesus sacrificed his good name to sit with sinners and save them.

And then there was the glory of his power to deliver people from demons. How shall this great goodness be destroyed? The fact that people were being freed by Jesus from demonic oppression was undeniable. It was a fact. But hatred for the truth is not easily defeated by facts. Facts simply give shape to the form of deceit. "He casts out demons by the prince of demons" (Matthew 9:34, RSV). "You are a Samaritan and have a demon" (John 8:48). "He has a demon, and he is mad; why listen to him?" (John 10:20, RSV). That was the best that they could do: Satan casting out Satan.

But what a truth the Lord released in response to this slander! A "house divided against itself will not stand" (Matthew 12:25). So even the slander is good news. But the truth is better: "The kingdom of God has come upon you. . . . How can anyone enter the strong man's house and carry off his property, unless he first binds the strong man? And then he will plunder his house" (Matthew 12:28-29). Behind the vilification of Christ is the manifestation of the kingdom of God. The "strong man" has been bound by one infinitely stronger. The goods are being plundered and the captives set free.

In this case, the devils know better than the Pharisees: "A man with an unclean spirit . . . cried out, 'What have you to do with us, Jesus of Nazareth? . . . I know who you are, the Holy One of God'" (Mark 1:23-24, RSV). Jesus does not cast out demons by the prince of demons. He rules the demons as the Holy One of God.

On and on the slanders go. "This man is not from God, because He does not keep the Sabbath" (John 9:16). "This man is a sinner" (John 9:24). "He has lost His senses" (Mark 3:21).

"He saved others; He cannot save Himself" (Matthew 27:42). "We heard Him say, 'I will destroy this temple made with hands, and in three days I will build another made without hands'" (Mark 14:58). But in every case, "wisdom is vindicated by her deeds" (Matthew 11:19). "If this man were not from God, He could do nothing" (John 9:33). "No one takes [my life] from me, but I lay it down of my own accord. I have power to lay it down, and I have power to take it again" (John 10:18, RSV).

In the end, the only "good name" that matters is not how men feel about us, but how God feels about us. The ultimate slander came on the cross. "Let God rescue Him now, if He delights in Him" (Matthew 27:43). If? There is no question. "This is My beloved Son, in whom I am well-pleased" (Matthew 3:17). This is the only good name that matters in the end. This is true riches. This is the glory of Christ.

A P R A Y E R

Father in heaven, you are the only one whose judgment matters in the end. What men think of us can burden or brighten our days. But it is of little account in the end. A good name among people may be better than great riches now, but neither name nor riches will survive the fire of your crucible. Truth is all that will matter. Not money or man's opinion. This we have learned from your Son, Jesus. Oh, how we love his unswerving indifference to the approval of men.

We praise you that he was fixed on you as the polestar of his life. What men said did not sway him to the right or the left. His compass was fixed on you. We are grieved that men with our own sinful nature spoke so ill of him. We have seen our own corruption in their slander. Forgive us for all our participation in speaking evil of the Son of God, or speaking nothing. Fill our minds and our mouths, O Lord, with the truth of Christ that we may speak well of him. Forbid that we would add to the avalanche of error spoken about Christ in the world. Let our mouths be signals on a hill that Jesus is the Christ, the Son of God. Flesh and blood does not teach this to us; it is revealed from you, O Father, in heaven. Speak, O God, through your written Word with stone-cleaving power, and grant us to see the truth of Jesus everywhere. Bend our affections toward him. Blow away the bad reputation of the Lord wherever we speak. May your Son be glorified in everything we say! In his name we pray, amen.

Being reviled,

He did not revile in return;

while suffering,

He uttered no threats.

1 PETER 2:23

꧁

It was the will of the LORD

to bruise him;

he has put him to grief.

ISAIAH 53:10, RSV

꧁

The Incomparable Sufferings

The Anguish of Jesus Christ

❧

The agonies of God's Son were incomparable. No one ever suffered like this man. Through all eternity, we will contemplate the killing of the Son of God and sing, "Worthy is the Lamb that was slain" (Revelation 5:12).

Count Zinzendorf (1700-1760) and the Moravians developed a theology based on the wounds and blood of Jesus that some believe became lopsided in its focus on the "five wounds" of Christ. But we are not in danger today of any such excess preoccupation with the anguish of Jesus. So come and worship with me at the splendor of Christ's sufferings.

No one ever deserved suffering less, yet received so much. The stamp of God on this perfect life is found in two words: "without sin" (Hebrews 4:15). The only person in history who did not deserve to suffer, suffered most. He "committed no sin, nor was any deceit found in his mouth" (1 Peter 2:22). None of Jesus' pain was a penalty for his sin. He had no sin.

Therefore, no one has ever had a greater right to retaliate, but used it less. He had at his disposal infinite power to take revenge at any moment in his agony. "Do you think that I cannot appeal to My Father, and He will at once put at My disposal more than twelve legions of angels?" (Matthew 26:53). But he did not do it. When every judicial sentiment in the universe cried out "Unjust!" Jesus was silent. "He did not answer [Pilate] with regard to even a single charge" (Matthew 27:14). Nor did he refute false ridicule: "Being reviled, He did not revile in return; while suffering, He uttered no threats" (1 Peter 2:23). Nor did he defend himself in response to Herod's interrogation: "He answered him nothing" (Luke 23:9). No one has ever borne so much injustice with so little vengeance.

This was not because the torment was tolerable. If we had been forced to watch, we probably would have passed out. In the garden, "His sweat became like drops of blood, falling down upon the ground" (Luke 22:44). In the middle of the night, before the high priest, "they spat in His face and beat Him with their fists; and others slapped Him" (Matthew 26:67). Before the governor they "scourged" him (Matthew 27:26). Eusebius (about A.D. 300) described Roman scourging of Christians like this: "At one time they were torn by scourges down to deep-seated veins and arteries, so that the hidden contents of the recesses of their bodies, their entrails and organs, were exposed to sight."[1]

In his agony the soldiers toyed with him. They dressed him in mock robes of royalty. They began to "blindfold Him, and to beat Him with their fists, and to say to Him, 'Prophesy!' And the officers received Him with slaps in the face" (Mark

14:65). A crown of thorns was pressed down on his head—made worse by being driven into his skull with blows. "They kept beating His head with a reed, and spitting on Him, and kneeling and bowing before Him" (Mark 15:19). In this condition he was unable to carry his own cross (Matthew 27:32).

The torture and shame continued. He was stripped. His hands and feet were nailed to the cross (Acts 2:23; Psalm 22:16). The mockery was unrelenting through the terrible morning. "Hail, King of the Jews!" "You who are going to destroy the temple and rebuild it in three days, save Yourself! If You are the Son of God, come down from the cross" (Matthew 27:29, 40). Even one of the criminals was "hurling abuse at Him" (Luke 23:39).

It was a hideous death. "The wounds swelled about the rough nails, and the torn and lacerated tendons and nerves caused excruciating agony. The arteries of the head and stomach were surcharged with blood and a terrific throbbing headache ensued. . . . The victim of crucifixion literally died a thousand deaths. . . . The suffering was so frightful that 'even among the raging passions of war pity was sometimes excited.'"[2]

All of this came upon the "friend of sinners," not with brothers at his side, but utterly abandoned. Judas had betrayed him with a kiss (Luke 22:48). Peter had denied him three times (Matthew 26:75). "All the disciples left him and fled" (Matthew 26:56). And in the darkest hour of the history of the world, God the Father struck his own Son with our punishment. "We esteemed him stricken, smitten *by God*, and afflicted" (Isaiah 53:4, RSV). The only person in the world who truly knew God (Matthew 11:27) cried out, "My God, My God, why have You forsaken Me?" (Matthew 27:46).

Never before or since has there been such suffering, because, in all its dreadful severity, it was a suffering by design. It was planned by God the Father and embraced by God the Son. "It was the will of the LORD to bruise him; he has put him to grief" (Isaiah 53:10, RSV). Jesus "was delivered over by the predetermined plan and foreknowledge of God" (Acts 2:23). Herod, Pilate, the soldiers, and the Jews did to Jesus "whatever [God's] hand and . . . purpose predestined to occur" (Acts 4:28). Down to the details, the sufferings of the Son were written in the Scriptures. "Jesus, knowing that all things had already been accomplished, *to fulfill the Scripture*, said, 'I am thirsty'" (John 19:28).

Not only was it suffering by design, but also by obedience. Jesus embraced the pain. He chose it—"obedient to the point of death, even death on a cross" (Philippians 2:8). And his obedience was sustained by faith in his Father. "When he suffered, he did not threaten; but he trusted to him who judges justly" (1 Peter 2:23, RSV). "Father, into Your hands I commit My spirit" (Luke 23:46).

In that faith he "set his face to go to Jerusalem" (Luke 9:51, RSV). Why? "For it cannot be that a prophet would perish outside of Jerusalem" (Luke 13:33). He had set his face to die. "What shall I say, 'Father, save Me from this hour'? But for this purpose I came to this hour" (John 12:27). He lived in order to die.

Therefore, the suffering and weakness of Jesus were a work

of his sovereign power. "No one takes [my life] from me, but I lay it down of my own accord" (John 10:18, RSV). He freely chose to join the Father's design for his own suffering and death.

And what was that design? To be a substitute for us, so that we might live. "The Son of Man [came] . . . to give His life a ransom for many" (Mark 10:45). "He himself bore our sins in His body on the cross" (1 Peter 2:24). "The LORD has laid on him the iniquity of us all" (Isaiah 53:6, RSV).

And the goal of it all? "Greater love has no man than this, that a man lay down his life for his friends" (John 15:13, RSV). Yes, but to what end? What does love pursue? Two great purposes were accomplished in the suffering of Christ, which are really one purpose. First, "Christ . . . died for sins once for all, the just for the unjust, *so that he might bring us to God*" (1 Peter 3:18). The suffering of Jesus brought us to God who is fullness of joy and pleasure forevermore. Second, in the very hour of death the Father and the Son were glorified. "Now is the Son of Man glorified, and God is glorified in Him" (John 13:31). Our joy in savoring God and his glory in saving us are one. That is the glory of Christ's incomparable sufferings.

A P R A Y E R

Father, what can we say? We feel utterly unworthy in the face of Christ's unspeakable sufferings. We are sorry. It was our sin that brought this to pass. It was we who struck him and spit on him and mocked him. O

Father, we are so sorry. We bow ourselves to the dirt and shut the mouths of our small, dark, petty, sinful souls. O Father, touch us with fresh faith that we might believe the incredible. That the very pain of Christ that makes us despair is our salvation. Open our fearful hearts to receive the Gospel. Waken dead parts of our hearts that cannot feel what must be felt—that we are loved with the deepest, strongest, purest love in the universe. Oh, grant us to have the power to comprehend with all the saints the height and depth and length and breadth of the love of Christ that surpasses knowledge, and may we be filled with all the fullness of God. Fight for us, O God, that we not drift numb and blind and foolish into vain and empty excitements. Life is too short, too precious, too painful to waste on worldly bubbles that burst. Heaven is too great, hell is too horrible, eternity is too long that we should putter around on the porch of eternity. O God, open our eyes to the vastness of the sufferings of Christ and what they mean for sin and holiness and hope and heaven. We fear our bent to trifling. Make us awake to the weight of glory—the glory of Christ's incomparable sufferings. In his great and wonderful name, amen.

"[Christ] commands even

the unclean spirits,

and they obey Him."

MARK 1:27

❧

He himself likewise

partook of the same nature,

that through death he might destroy him

who has the power of death,

that is, the devil.

HEBREWS 2:14, RSV

❧

9

THE GLORY OF RESCUING SINNERS, NOT REMOVING SATAN

The Saving Sacrifice of Jesus Christ

❧

The glory of Christ is seen in his absolute right and power to annihilate or incapacitate Satan and all demons. But the reason he refrains from destroying and disabling them altogether is to manifest more clearly his superior beauty and worth. If Christ obliterated all devils and demons now (which he could do), his sheer power would be seen as glorious, but his superior beauty and worth would not shine as brightly as when humans renounce the promises of Satan and take pleasure in the greater glory of Christ.

The devil and his angels are irredeemable. Jesus implies this when he says that "eternal fire . . . has been prepared for the devil and his angels" (Matthew 25:41). And Jude confirms it when he says that the fallen angels are being "kept in eternal bonds under darkness for the judgment of the great day" (verse 6). Therefore, the reason Christ withholds his judgment from them now is *not* to give them a chance to repent and be saved.

Then why not obliterate them altogether, or at least paralyze their harmful influence? Is it because they have free will (in the sense of ultimate self-determination) and Christ cannot stop them? No. Too many texts illustrate the right and power of Christ to restrain and remove Satan and his demons. For example, 1) "[Christ] commands even the unclean spirits, and they obey Him" (Mark 1:27). 2) When Satan does act in freedom, it is only by divine permission. "Simon, Simon, behold, Satan has asked permission to sift you like wheat; but I have prayed for you, that your faith may not fail" (Luke 22:31-32). 3) Even though Paul's "thorn in the flesh" is a "messenger of Satan," nevertheless Christ makes it serve Paul's humility and the display of Christ's own power (2 Corinthians 12:7-10). 4) In the end, God will bind Satan for a thousand years, then, finally, throw him into the lake of fire (Revelation 20:2, 10). Therefore, the decision to leave Satan in the world is not because Christ does not have the right and power to remove him. What, then, is the reason?

Christ must have a very high stake in the ongoing existence of Satan, because, even though he has the right and power to annihilate him now, he defeats him in stages at the cost of his own life. "The Son of God appeared for this purpose, to destroy the works of the devil" (1 John 3:8). But *how* did he do this? Hebrews 2:14 gives one answer: "He himself likewise partook of the same [human] nature, that *through death* he might destroy him who has the power of death, that is, the devil" (RSV). In other words, Christ became human so that he could die, and by dying "destroy" the devil.

This means that Christ's aim in defeating the devil must be something different from the mere removal of Satan's deadly influence. He could have accomplished that with one command: "Go to hell!" And the devil would have obeyed—as one day he will! What then is the kind of defeat Christ achieved over Satan? And why is it superior to the simple removal of Satan out of history?

The key is that Satan is defeated by the *death* of Jesus. Paul puts it this way, referring to the death of Christ: "When He had disarmed the rulers and authorities [by the death of Christ], He made a public display of them, having triumphed over them through Him" (Colossians 2:15). In what sense did he disarm Satan's "rulers and authorities"? Satan still blinds (2 Corinthians 4:4) and tempts (1 Thessalonians 3:5) and deceives (Revelation 20:3) and casts into prison (Revelation 2:10) and takes captive (2 Timothy 2:26) and destroys flesh (1 Corinthians 5:5). He does not *look* disarmed or destroyed. How then is he disarmed by the death of Jesus?

One answer is that the death of Jesus nullified the damning effect of sin for all who trust in Christ. The weapon of soul-destroying sin and guilt is taken out of Satan's hand. He is disarmed of the single weapon that can condemn us—unforgiven sin. We see this in 1 Corinthians 15:55-57: "O death, where is your victory? O death, where is your sting? The sting of death is sin, and the power of sin is the law; but thanks be to God, who gives us the victory through our Lord Jesus Christ." Why is *sin* the sting of death? Because only unforgiven sin can condemn the soul and make death a door to hell, not heaven.

Therefore, the way that Satan can destroy the soul is not by seances or apparitions or sickness or persecution, but only by securing the guilt of our sin. "But thanks be to God," Paul says, "who gives us the victory through our Lord Jesus Christ."

"Christ also died for sins once for all, the just for the unjust, so that He might bring us to God" (1 Peter 3:18). If our sins are forgiven for Christ's sake, Satan has no damning weapon against us. He can hurt us, and even kill us, but he cannot condemn us. This is what Hebrews 2:14 meant when it said that by death Christ "destroyed the one who has the power of death" (RSV). Satan had the "power of death" in the sense that he wielded the lethal "sting of death." But now by the blood of Christ our sins are forgiven, and Satan's soul-destroying power is nullified for all who are in Christ. There is no condemnation—from Satan or anyone.

You can see it again in the words "The sting of death is sin, and *the power of sin is the law*" (1 Corinthians 15:56). If *sin* is the lethal sting of death, it is so because the *law* fixes an eternal penalty for sin. "The wages of sin is [eternal] death" (Romans 6:23). But when Christ died as our perfect substitute, Paul says that God "canceled the bond which stood against us with its legal demands; this he set aside, nailing it to the cross" (Colossians 2:14, RSV). So the weapon of the law was taken out of Satan's hand. He cannot use it to condemn the people of God.

Now without *sin* and *law* to condemn and accuse and oppress us, Satan is a defeated foe. He is disarmed. Christ has triumphed over him, not by putting him out of existence, but by letting him live and watch while millions of saints find forgiveness for their sins and turn their back on Satan because of the greater glory of the grace of Christ.

It was a costly triumph. But God's values are not so easily reckoned. If God had simply terminated Satan, then it would not have been so clear that God is *both* stronger *and* infinitely more to be desired than Satan. God wills for his glory to shine forth not only through acts of physical power, but also through acts of moral and spiritual power that display the beauty of his grace with lavish colors. To take sinners out of Satan's hands by virtue of Christ's sin-bearing sacrifice and his law-fulfilling obedience to the Father was a more glorious victory than mere annihilation of the enemy.

A PRAYER

Heavenly Father, we are sobered that you would regard the glory of your Son so highly that it would be worth the ongoing existence of Satan to make it fully known. We are ashamed that we have murmured about the battles of life when we should have made every effort to magnify your Christ-exalting reasons for giving the enemy so much leash. Forgive us for failing to see your holy purposes. And now, O God, by the blood of your Son, our Savior, give us victory over Satan. Grant us to see and savor the superior worth of Christ. Let us shame Satan by making much of

Jesus. Grant us to glory in the work of the cross. Help us to cherish the finished work of Christ that disarmed Satan and took the sting out of death. Teach us how to fight by faith against the power of sin, in the confidence that Christ has purchased our forgiveness and secured the triumph of all who trust in him. Turn every evil design of the devil into sanctifying schemes of love. Deliver us from his deceptions. Keep the beauty of Christ clear in the eyes of our heart. Make us instruments of Satan's defeat until you come and slay him by the breath of your mouth. Make us valiant in delivering others by the sword of the Spirit, the Word of God, your great Gospel. In Jesus' name we pray, amen.

But God, being rich in mercy,

because of His great love with which He loved us,

even when we were dead in our transgressions,

made us alive together with Christ.

EPHESIANS 2:4-5

❧

Therefore let us draw near

with confidence to the throne of grace,

so that we may receive mercy

and find grace to help in time of need.

HEBREWS 4:16

❧

10

THE INCARNATE WEALTH OF THE COMPASSION OF GOD

The Mercies of Jesus Christ

❧

God is the wealthiest person in the universe. He not only owns more than anyone else. He owns everyone else and everything everyone else owns. When you create something, it belongs to you. And God created everything—including us. "It is He who has made us, and not we ourselves; we are His people and the sheep of His pasture" (Psalm 100:3). There is one ultimate owner in the universe, God. All others are trustees. Neither we nor what we have is finally our own. It is all a trust to be used for the aims of the owner. In a sense, therefore, all sin is embezzling.

But, strikingly, the New Testament describes the wealth of God not mainly in terms of what he created and owns, but mainly in terms of the glory he has from all eternity. Repeatedly we read of "the riches of His glory" or "His riches in glory" (for example, Ephesians 3:16; Philippians 4:19; Colossians 1:27). If God were only rich because he made and owns all things, he would have been poor before creation. But that means he would have created out of need and would be dependent on his creation. But that is not the picture of God we find in the Bible. God did not create to get wealth; he created to display wealth—the wealth of his glory for the enjoyment of his people (Ephesians 1:6, 12, 14).

But even more specifically, the focus of the New Testament is that the wealth of God's glory is, at its apex, the wealth of his mercy. This is something the world takes very lightly: "the riches of [God's] kindness and forbearance and patience" (Romans 2:4, RSV). God created and redeemed the world so that he might "make known the riches of His glory upon vessels of mercy, which He prepared beforehand for glory" (Romans 9:23). Or, to put it another way, he creates and saves his people "in order that in the ages to come He might show the surpassing riches of His grace in kindness toward us in Christ Jesus" (Ephesians 2:7). The universe exists primarily to display the wealth of the glory of the mercy of God for the enjoyment of his redeemed people from every tribe and tongue and people and nation.

Justice is essential among the perfections of God's glory. But mercy is paramount. "He who justifies the wicked, and he who condemns the righteous . . . are an abomination to the LORD" (Proverbs 17:15). Yes. Therefore justice is essential. But something else is also true: "It is [a man's] glory to overlook a transgression" (Proverbs 19:11). Therefore, if justice can be preserved, it is the apex of glory to show mercy.

For this reason Jesus Christ came into the world. Jesus is

the mercy of God incarnate and visible. He is also the justice of God incarnate; but justice was subordinate: "God did not send the Son into the world to judge the world, but that the world might be saved through Him" (John 3:17). God the Father offered up his Son in death so "that He would be just and the justifier of the one who has faith in Jesus" (Romans 3:26). The substitutionary death of Jesus Christ created the backdrop of justice where justifying mercy would shine with unparalleled glory. Therefore, the glory of God's mercy is the aim of Christ's coming. This is explicit in Romans 15:8-9: Christ came into the world "to confirm the promises given to the fathers, and *for the Gentiles to glorify God for His mercy.*" The aim of the incarnation was to magnify the mercy of God for the enjoyment of the nations.

In Mary's *Magnificat,* and in Zechariah's prophetic song at the birth of John the Baptist, the reason given for the coming of Jesus was "in remembrance of [God's] mercy" (Luke 1:54), and "because of the tender mercy of our God" (Luke 1:78). Or as the apostle Paul put it, the work of Christ is due to God's being "rich in mercy" (Ephesians 2:4). It is all "according to the riches of His grace" (Ephesians 1:7). He is "abounding in riches for all who call on Him" (Romans 10:12).

This mercy that Jesus embodies and brings is utterly free. Not that there was no cost. Jesus paid the price at the cost of his own life. "In Him we have redemption *through His blood,* the forgiveness of our trespasses, according to the riches of His grace" (Ephesians 1:7). But now, to broken and needy sinners, it is absolutely free. Thus God says, "'I will have mercy on whom I have mercy, and I will have compassion on whom I have compassion.' So then it does not depend on the man who wills or the man who runs, but on God who has mercy. . . . So then He has mercy on whom He desires, and He hardens whom He desires" (Romans 9:14-16, 18). We do not earn mercy. We receive it as a free gift by faith, not by works. "He saved us, not on the basis of deeds which we have done in righteousness, but according to His mercy" (Titus 3:5).

Even the faith to receive this mercy is itself a gift of mercy. "To you it has been freely given for Christ's sake to believe" (Philippians 1:29, author's translation). And what about others? Let us correct "those who are in opposition, if perhaps *God may grant them repentance* leading to the knowledge of the truth" (2 Timothy 2:25; see also Ephesians 2:8; John 6:44; Acts 13:48). From start to finish, God saves us "not according to our works, but according to His own purpose and grace which was granted us in Christ Jesus from all eternity" (2 Timothy 1:9). His triumphant mercy is utterly free.

Since Christ is the incarnate display of the wealth of the mercies of God, it is not surprising that his life on earth was a lavish exhibit of mercies to all kinds of people. Every kind of need and pain was touched by the mercies of Jesus in his few years on earth.

When the blind beggar cried out, "Jesus, Son of David, have mercy on me!" many were embarrassed and indignant. But "Jesus said to him, 'Receive your sight; your faith has made you well'" (Luke 18:38, 42).

When the revolting and feared lepers raised their voices and said, "Jesus, Master, have mercy on us!" he stopped and took pity on them and said, "'Go and show yourselves to the priests.' And as they were going, they were cleansed" (Luke 17:13-14). Even more remarkably, Mark recalls the time another dreaded leper fell on his knees pleading with Jesus to make him clean, and Jesus not only spoke to him, but also touched him: "Moved with compassion, Jesus stretched out His hand and touched him, and said to him, 'I am willing; be cleansed'" (Mark 1:41).

When Jesus saw a widow who had not only lost her husband but now her only son as well, Luke tells us, "[Jesus] felt compassion for her, and said to her, 'Do not weep'" (Luke 7:13). Then he raised her son from the dead. And in this case, not a word was said about her faith. It was a free and lavish overflow of divine mercy, even before faith.

Mercy also drew Jesus to those who were made miserable by demons. One man brought his demon-possessed son to Jesus after years of sorrow. The boy was unable to speak, and the evil spirit often threw the boy into the fire. The father pleaded with Jesus, "Take pity on us and help us!" (Mark 9:22). And even though the grieving father could only manage a mustard seed of faith—"I do believe; help my unbelief" (Mark 9:24)— Jesus responded to the cry for pity and rebuked the spirit and cast it out.

Even when a demon-possessed man had no one to be his advocate and could not believe or submit to Jesus—as in the case of the Gerasene demoniac—the Lord delivered him and then explained that it was sheer mercy: "Go home to your people and report to them what great things the Lord has done for you, and how He had mercy on you" (Mark 5:19). And don't miss the added mercy that this man was not a Jew, but a foreigner just like the "Canaanite woman" who cried out, "Have mercy on me, Lord, Son of David; my daughter is cruelly demon-possessed" (Matthew 15:22). Neither the demons nor the Gentile distance from Israel stopped the mercy of Jesus.

Not only was the mercy of Jesus kindled by suffering, but also by sin. When Jesus ate with "tax collectors and sinners," the Pharisees and scribes criticized him. But Jesus told three parables to explain what he was doing. One was the parable of the prodigal son. The climax of this parable pictures God, filled with compassion for his sin-soaked, home-coming son: "While [the son] was still a long way off, his father saw him and felt compassion for him, and ran and embraced him and kissed him" (Luke 15:20). In other words, Jesus ate with tax collectors and sinners because he was the incarnate display of the Father's tender compassion for sinners.

Jesus showed this compassion not only for individuals who sin and suffer, but also for whole multitudes. He did not look on masses with contempt or with impersonal indifference. Once when great crowds had followed him and had not planned well for their food, Jesus looked on them and said, "I feel compassion for the people because they have remained with Me now three days and have nothing to eat" (Mark 8:2). On another occasion, it was not their hunger but their spiritual need for truth that filled him with compassion for the crowds: "He saw a large crowd, and He felt compassion for them because they were like sheep without a shepherd; and He began to teach them many things" (Mark 6:34).

One of the most sweeping statements about God's mercy that Jesus ever made came from Hosea 6:6. It was Jesus' way of putting the whole Old Testament ceremonial law under the banner of mercy instead of meticulous rules. When he was criticized for going to dinner at Matthew's house with unclean tax collectors, he turned the criticism around and said, "Go and learn what this means:, 'I desire compassion, and not sacrifice' [Hosea 6:6], for I did not come to call the righteous, but sinners" (Matthew 9:13). And when his disciples were rebuked by the Pharisees for picking grain and eating it on the Sabbath, Jesus said, "If you had known what this means, 'I desire compassion, and not a sacrifice,' you would not have condemned the innocent" (Matthew 12:7). In other words, Jesus' entire ministry was shaped by the insight that mercy is the ultimate meaning of God's law. And since Jesus came not to abolish but to fulfill that law (Matthew 5:17), he was the incarnation and manifestation of the wealth of the mercy of God.

The same is true of Jesus today. In this regard "Jesus Christ is the same yesterday and today and forever" (Hebrews 13:8). This is why God, who is called "the Father of mercies" (2 Corinthians 1:3), beckons us to come boldly to his throne through Jesus Christ who can "sympathize with our weaknesses" (Hebrews 4:15). Jesus is our sinless, all-sufficient High Priest. He has offered himself as our substitute in perfect obedience and perfect sacrifice. All the Father's mercies belong to those who come to God through faith in Jesus. "Therefore let

us draw near with confidence to the throne of grace, so that
we may receive mercy and may find grace to help in time of
need" (Hebrews 4:16).

The place where mercies are kept is at the throne of God.
Here is infinite wealth and infinite power and infinite wisdom. And all this stands ready in the service of mercy, because
of Jesus Christ, the mercy of God incarnate. Whether you learn
this through pleasure, or learn it through pain, like Job, whatever you do, learn it: "The Lord is full of compassion and is
merciful" (James 5:11).

A P R A Y E R

*O Father, how we need mercy. We sin every day. We
fall short of your command to love you with all our
heart and soul and mind and strength. We are luke-
warm in our affections. All our motives, even at their
best, are mixed. We murmur. We are anxious about
tomorrow. We get angry too quickly. We desire what
ought not be desired. We get irritated at the very atti-
tudes in others that we ourselves displayed five minutes
before. If you do not show mercy to us, we are undone.
O God, let us see the mercy of Christ and savor it for
what it is. Grant us power to comprehend his love.
Incline us to read and ponder the stories of the mercy
of Jesus in the Gospels. Let us so admire what he did
that we imitate him. But let it be much more than*

external imitation. Let it come from the heart where we have been broken for our sin and where we have come to cherish mercy and live by mercy and hope in mercy and long for mercy. Make the mercy of Jesus the greatest beauty of the Savior in our eyes. Let us behold, and beholding, become like him. And bend this taste for mercy outward so that we show it. Make us full of his mercy that we might show mercy. Fulfill in us the command to do justice and love mercy. Let us love showing mercy. Make it so much a part of us that it is who we are. So unite us to Christ that his mercy is our mercy, and our mercy is a presenting of Christ. He is all we have to give in the end. Glorify his mercy, Father, in our faith and in our patience. Thank you, oh, thank you, for Christ and your mercy to us in him. In his name we pray, amen.

"Teacher, we know that . . .

You are not partial to any, but teach

the way of God in truth."

LUKE 20:21

⚘

"I praise You, O Father,

Lord of heaven and earth,

that You have hidden these things

from the wise and intelligent

and have revealed them to infants."

LUKE 10:21

⚘

11

THE TOUGH SIDE

The Severity of Jesus Christ

&

The glory of Jesus Christ is that he is always out of sync with the world and therefore always relevant for the world. If he fit nicely, he would be of little use. The effort to remake the Jesus of the Bible so that he fits the spirit of one generation makes him feeble in another. Better to let him be what he is, because it is often the offensive side of Jesus that we need most.

Especially offensive to the modern, western sentiment is the tough, blunt, fierce form of Jesus' love. People with thin skin would often have felt hurt by Jesus' piercing tongue. People who identify love only with soft and tender words and ways would have been repeatedly outraged by the stinging, almost violent, language of the Lord.

Not that this was the only way he spoke. We have seen the sweetness of his mercies and how patient and kind and forgiving he was (Chapter 10). That is why his severe speech cannot be written off as peevishness or as flares of temper or callous hostility. What we meet in the biting language of Christ is a form of love that corresponds with the real world of corruption and the dullness of our hearts and the magnitude of what is at stake in our choices. If there were no great evils and no deaf hearts and no eternal consequences, perhaps the only fitting forms of love would be a soft touch and tender words. But such a world does not kill the Son of God and hate his disciples. There is no such world.

We need to listen to the stunning severity of Jesus' mercy. It caused people to marvel in his own day. Even his enemies admitted that he was amazingly indifferent to the approval of others. We tend to be overly concerned that others approve of how we speak. Jesus was not. "Teacher, we know that . . . You are not partial to any, but teach the way of God in truth" (Luke 20:21). When the hostile Pharisees sent officers to seize Jesus, they came back empty-handed with this explanation: "Never has a man spoken the way this man speaks" (John 7:46).

That has been the testimony of every generation. No man ever spoke like this man. It began when he was a boy in the temple: "All who heard Him were amazed at . . . His answers" (Luke 2:47). When he entered his public ministry in the synagogue in Nazareth, at first "all were speaking well of Him, and wondering at the gracious words which were falling from His lips" (Luke 4:22); but when he bluntly cut across the grain of their self-centered expectations (verses 24-27), the same people "were filled with rage" (verse 28) and tried to throw him off a cliff (verse 29). Then, at the end of his ministry in the last week of his life, his piercing answers finally stopped the mouths of his adversaries, except for the cry of condemnation. "No one was able to answer Him a word, nor did anyone dare from that day on to ask Him another question" (Matthew 22:46).

The condition of the world that made the coming of Christ necessary was so bad that Jesus reached for shocking language to capture it. When people came asking for a sign he responded, "An evil and adulterous generation seeks after a sign" (Matthew 16:4). When his own disciples could not cast out a demon he said, "O unbelieving generation, how long shall I be with you? How long shall I put up with you?" (Mark 9:19). When he taught them to pray, he said, "If you then, *being evil*, know how to give good gifts to your children, how much more will your Father who is in heaven give what is good to those who ask Him!" (Matthew 7:11). He started with the assumption that they were evil, and he told them so.

Not only did Jesus indict the world as evil and adulterous and unbelieving, he said that all were spiritually dead. When a disciple asked Jesus if he could go bury his father, Jesus shocked him with the words, "Follow Me, and allow the dead to bury their own dead" (Matthew 8:22). A terrible condition of living death called for tough words. It was the same with the Pharisees: "Woe to you! For you are like concealed tombs" (Luke 11:44). "You are like whitewashed tombs which on the outside appear beautiful, but inside they are full of dead men's bones" (Matthew 23:27).

The deadness was satanic because Satan has been a spiritual murderer of man from the beginning. Jesus outraged pious unbelievers with this incrimination: "You are of your father the devil, and you want to do the desires of your father. He was a murderer from the beginning, and does not stand in the truth" (John 8:44). And when his own devoted disciple Peter spoke heroically about not letting Jesus be killed, Jesus turned to him and said, "Get behind Me, Satan! You are a stumbling block to Me" (Matthew 16:23). There was one solution to spiritual death: Jesus' substitutionary death. Any hindrance to that was demonic. No words were too strong to repel it.

The condition of the human heart will lead to eternal punishment for those who do not receive the remedy Christ brought. Therefore Jesus spared no delicate feelings in warning against hell. No one in the Bible spoke more often, or more frightfully, about hell: "The angels will come forth and take out the wicked from among the righteous, and will throw them into the furnace of fire; in that place there will be weeping and gnashing of teeth" (Matthew 13:49-50). When his disciples tried to pin Jesus down about the place of judgment, he simply answered, "Where the body is, there also the vultures will be gathered" (Luke 17:37). Some realities are so fearful, they don't call for specific precision but scandalous portrayal.

Hell, Jesus said, is a place "where their worm does not die, and the fire is not quenched" (Mark 9:48). It is a place of "outer darkness" (Matthew 8:12; 22:13; 25:30). It is "eternal fire which has been prepared for the devil and his angels" (Matthew 25:41). The fire is "unquenchable" (Mark 9:43). It is "eternal punishment" (Matthew 25:46).

Therefore, Jesus explains with heart-stopping reasonable-

ness that mere earthly dangers—like being killed!—are as nothing compared to the danger of hell: "I say to you, My friends,
do not be afraid of those who kill the body, and after that have
no more that they can do. But I will warn you whom to fear:
fear the One who, after He has killed, has authority to cast
into hell; yes, I tell you, fear Him!" (Luke 12:4-5). In other
words, "Fear not, my disciples, you can only be killed!"

It follows, starkly, that horrific calamities in this world, no
matter how painful, are not the greatest tragedy. Far greater is
the failure to escape hell through repentance and faith. Jesus
had a very unsentimental way of speaking this utterly crucial
truth to people who put their worst horrors in the wrong place.
For example, one group was horrified at Pilate's mingling the
blood of some Galilean worshipers with their sacrifices. They
reported this suffering to Jesus, who must have astonished them
when he said, "Do you suppose that these Galileans were
greater sinners than all other Galileans because they suffered
this fate? I tell you, no, but unless you repent, you will all likewise perish" (Luke 13:2-3). In other words, instead of being
amazed that sinful humans perish, be amazed that you haven't.

Jesus will show us the way to heaven whether we can stomach it or not. "If your right eye makes you stumble, tear it out
and throw it from you; for it is better for you to lose one of
the parts of your body, than for your whole body to be thrown
into hell. If your right hand makes you stumble, cut it off and
throw it from you; for it is better for you to lose one of the parts
of your body, than for your whole body to go into hell"
(Matthew 5:29-30). Better self-mutilation than damnation.

So it is with our own damnation, and how much more with the damnation of others: "Whoever causes one of these little ones who believe in Me to stumble, it is better for him to have a heavy millstone hung around his neck, and to be drowned in the depth of the sea" (Matthew 18:6). Better to perish in the sea than to push another into hell.

So it is not surprising that Jesus would describe entering the kingdom as an act of violence: "From the days of John the Baptist until now the kingdom of heaven suffers violence, and violent men take it by force" (Matthew 11:12). And it is not surprising that he would say, "The gate is small and the way is narrow that leads to life, and there are few who find it" (Matthew 7:14). There are not many who will trust Christ so deeply and cherish heaven so dearly that they count their eyes and hands and lives less precious than fellowship with Jesus in Paradise. So the way is narrow, and few follow. Rather, many listen to Jesus and say, "This is a difficult statement; who can listen to it?" (John 6:60).

But he doesn't let up. He presses for a narrow way not only in regard to our hands and eyes being pure, and our love for babes being radical; he also takes aim at our undue allegiance to family and self and possessions. "If anyone comes to Me, and does not hate his own father and mother and wife and children and brothers and sisters, yes, and even his own life, he cannot be My disciple" (Luke 14:26). "He who hates his life in this world will keep it to life eternal" (John 12:25). "None of you can be My disciple who does not give up all his own possessions" (Luke 14:33). Even love for godly parents will often look like hate to the world when we seek the kingdom first. And if our parents are not godly, the very faith that makes us seek their salvation will turn them against us: "I came to set a man against his father, and a daughter against her mother, and a daughter-in-law against her mother-in-law" (Matthew 10:35). Do we then lose our family when we follow Christ? Jesus' answer comes out of the blue: "Whoever does the will of My Father who is in heaven, he is My brother and sister and mother" (Matthew 12:50).

If this does not sound like the ministry of the Prince of Peace, realize that his aim is not peace with unbelief and disobedience. Those are the enemies that must be destroyed, lest they destroy. When the amnesty of Jesus is despised, division is inevitable—and he knew it: "Do you suppose that I came to grant peace on earth? I tell you, no, but rather division" (Luke 12:51). "You will be betrayed even by parents and brothers and relatives and friends, and they will put some of you to death" (Luke 21:16). "I have come to cast fire upon the earth; and how I wish it were already kindled!" (Luke 12:49).

Who can hear these things? Who can rejoice in these words and penetrate to the truth of Jesus' words when he says, "These things I have spoken to you so that My joy may be in you, and that your joy may be made full" (John 15:11)? Jesus' answer is as surprising as the language that raised the question. And he gives it with joy: "He rejoiced greatly in the Holy Spirit, and said, 'I praise You, O Father, Lord of heaven and earth, that You have hidden these things from the wise and intelligent and have revealed them to infants'" (Luke 10:21).

The humble, the teachable, the broken, the submissive—
the babes—these will hear the voice of strength and truth
and righteousness and love. They will hear, and their hearts
will burn within them when he speaks (Luke 24:32). They will
not be offended. They will take heart that at last someone
sees the severity of our human condition, knows the enemy,
will not compromise, and speaks like a conquering King and
a great Savior.

A P R A Y E R

*Lord, thicken our skin. Not that we be less tender,
but that we be less easily offended. Take away our bent
to self-pity. Give us a passion for the truth that is
stronger than our inborn passion for being praised.
Forgive us, Father, for calling words unloving just
because they were tough. Forgive us for attributing
malicious motives to people when we don't know their
motives. Help us to learn from Jesus when to be tough
and when to be tender. Guard us from justifying
merely human anger with the hard sayings of Jesus.
But don't let us become so mushy that we can't speak
a firm word in season. We marvel at the words of our
Lord Jesus. How unpredictable he was! No one ever
spoke like he did. He is in a class by himself. We bow
before him and shut our mouths. We are eager for him
to speak—and to speak any way he pleases. We are*

the silent learners. He is the sinless teacher. We put our hands upon our mouths and take our place at his feet. Do with us as you please, Father. We are not your judge, nor the judge of how your Son speaks. Have mercy on us—tough or tender—and lead us to your everlasting joy. In the name of your Son, our Lord Jesus, amen.

Christ, having been raised from the dead,

is never to die again;

death no longer is master over Him.

ROMANS 6:9

꙳

[God] raised Him from the dead

and gave Him glory.

1 PETER 1:21

꙳

12

INVINCIBLE LIFE

The Resurrection of Jesus Christ

⚜

God raised Jesus Christ from the dead (1 Corinthians 15:4; 1 Peter 1:21). Everybody knew he was dead, from the governor to the executing soldiers to the women who buried him to the adversaries who feared a conspiracy of resurrection rumor. They all knew he was dead. That is why the fabrication concocted to explain the empty tomb was not that he wasn't really dead, but that the disciples stole the body (Matthew 28:13). But it didn't work, because people don't risk their lives for a self-made falsehood. The body was not in the tomb, otherwise the enemies would have put a stop to Christianity with Jesus' remains. The disciples were ablaze with boldness, risking their lives by preaching that Jesus was alive (Acts 2:24, 32; 3:15). The evangelist Stephen and the apostle James lost their lives (Acts 7:60; 12:2). And for forty days Jesus was appearing to individuals and groups, some as large as five hundred (Acts 1:3; 1 Corinthians 15:6). Most of these were not gullible, but hard to convince (Luke 24:11, 38; John 20:25, 27).

As the possibility dawned on the skeptical disciples that the resurrection might be true, the first speculation was that the Jesus they saw was a ghost or apparition of some kind. But Jesus was ruthless to abolish this speculation immediately. To doubting Thomas he said, "Reach here with your finger, and see My hands; and reach here your hand and put it into My side; and do not be unbelieving, but believing" (John 20:27). And before the stunned disciples on another occasion, Jesus insisted on eating fish to show them that he was not a ghost. "'See My hands and My feet, that it is I Myself; touch Me and see, for a spirit does not have flesh and bones as you see that I have.' . . . While they still could not believe it because of their joy and amazement, He said to them, 'Have you anything here to eat?' They gave Him a piece of a broiled fish; and He took it and ate it before them" (Luke 24:39-43).

But Jesus' resurrection body was more than a merely resuscitated mortal body. It was the same and yet not the same. He could be recognized as the one he always was. His body was a physical body. But it was also a transformed body. When the apostle Paul described the future resurrection body of Christians, he was describing the resurrection body of Jesus too, because Christ was raised as "the first fruits" of the rest of the dead who belong to him (1 Corinthians 15:20). In other words, the body of the risen Christ is part of the same harvest of all the other bodies that he will raise in glory at the last day. Christ, Paul says, "will transform the body of our humble state into conformity with the body of His glory" (Philippians 3:21). Therefore this description of our future resurrection bodies applies to Jesus' body too: "It is sown a perishable body, it is raised an imperishable body; it is sown in dishonor, it is raised in glory; it is sown in weakness, it is raised in power; it is sown a natural body, it is raised a spiritual body" (1 Corinthians 15:42-44). It is the same and yet gloriously superior.

Tremendous divine power preceded, accompanied, and followed the resurrection of Jesus. Leading up to his resurrection, Jesus was utterly in charge of his living and dying. "I lay down My life so that I may take it again. No one has taken it away from Me, but I lay it down on My own initiative. I have authority to lay it down, and I have authority to take it up again" (John 10:17-18). Jesus scoffed at threats that he could be brought to death before his hour, much less that he could be held in the tomb beyond his own will. When warned that Herod wanted to kill him, Jesus said, "Go and tell that fox, 'Behold, I cast out demons and perform cures today and tomorrow, and the third day I reach My goal'" (Luke 13:32). He predicted the details of his death and resurrection as one who was following his own unstoppable plan: "Jesus said to them, 'The Son of Man is going to be delivered into the hands of men; and they will kill Him, and He will be raised on the third day'" (Matthew 17:22-23).

In the very act of resurrection, divine power held complete sway. Paul referred to "the working of the strength of [God's] might which He brought about in Christ, when He raised Him from the dead" (Ephesians 1:19-20). And Peter said, "It was impossible for Him to be held in [death's] power" (Acts 2:24).

Coming through death with sovereign power, Christ entered into an imperishable, never-ending life. Jesus has become an ever-living High Priest "according to the power of an indestructible life" (Hebrews 7:16). "Christ, having been raised from the dead, is never to die again; death no longer is master over Him" (Romans 6:9). "God highly exalted Him, and bestowed on Him the name which is above every name" (Philippians 2:9). "[God] raised Him from the dead and gave Him glory" (1 Peter 1:21). Before, during, and afterwards, the resurrection of Jesus was a glorious manifestation of divine power.

Therefore the resurrection of Jesus assures all his future work on behalf of his people: his authority and rule over everything in the universe (Matthew 28:18); his priestly intercession on our behalf (Romans 8:34); his advocacy with God the Father (1 John 2:1); his protecting, comforting presence with us to the end of the age (Matthew 28:20); and his final coming to earth in glory to give rest to us and retribution to all who "do not know God and to those do not obey the gospel of our Lord Jesus" (2 Thessalonians 1:7-8).

And the resurrection of Jesus therefore secures all the blessings he obtained for us in his death. The resurrection vindicates the sufficiency of the cross and seals the certainty and finality of our justification by faith. "[Jesus] was delivered over because of our transgressions, and was raised because of our justification" (Romans 4:25). All the promises of God, purchased by the blood of Christ, become ours in everlasting perpetuity because of the resurrection of Jesus. Forgiveness, for example:

"If Christ has not been raised, your faith is worthless; you are still in your sins" (1 Corinthians 15:17). But he has been raised, and so forgiveness is real and permanent. "He always lives to make intercession for [us]" (Hebrews 7:25).

In the end, the risen Christ will raise us up with him. "If the Spirit of Him who raised Jesus from the dead dwells in you, He who raised Christ Jesus from the dead will also give life to your mortal bodies through His Spirit who dwells in you" (Romans 8:11). "If we have become united with Him in the likeness of His death, certainly we shall be also in the likeness of His resurrection" (Romans 6:5). Just as Jesus took back his own life from the fangs of death, so he will raise from the dead those who are his. He makes this promise for all who believe: "I Myself will raise him up on the last day" (John 6:40). Thus his resurrection guarantees theirs. They are secure in glory as he is. "They cannot even die anymore . . . being sons of the resurrection" (Luke 20:36). "Over these the second death has no power" (Revelation 20:6).

The glory of Christ in the power of his resurrection into invincible life and omnipotent authority will be reflected back to him in the joyful worship of his risen and perfected saints. Who shall enjoy this eternal gift of life? Jesus answers: "I am the resurrection and the life; he who believes in Me . . . will never die" (John 11:25-26).

Like every historical fact, the resurrection of Jesus can be doubted. But when God takes in hand the reliability of the witnesses, the courage of their preaching, the futility of the opposition, the effects of the Gospel, the coherence of the message, the all-embracing sufficiency of the Christian worldview, and the spiritual glory of Jesus Christ—when God takes all this and more in hand, he is able to open the mind of the most resistant skeptic. When God wakens us from the stupor of unbelief and shines into our mind with "the light of the gospel of the glory of Christ" (2 Corinthians 4:4, 6), what we see, along with the terrible splendor of his suffering, is the grandeur of his resurrection.

A PRAYER

Father of glory, we praise you that you mightily raised your Son, Jesus, from the dead. We praise you that the stone which the builders rejected has become the cornerstone. This is your doing and it is marvelous in our eyes. Death could not hold him! Our last enemy has fallen before your power in the triumph of Jesus over death, and we have been freed from fear of this ancient enemy. And now, O God, grant us to live in the riches of all that Jesus' resurrection means. All authority belongs to him in heaven and on earth. No power and no enemy can prevail against him. Only good can come to us in the end as we trust in him. The best is always yet to come. So, Father, banish fear and fretting and discouragement and moodiness from our lives. Rivet our attention on the ultimate reality of Christ's final triumph over death. Never let us forget or fail to feel universal glory that you have given Jesus a name that is above every name. Make this practical in our daily lives as we see every person, great and small, facing someday the risen and triumphant Judge of all the nations. Give us a brokenhearted boldness in the mercy and the might of Jesus. O Father, we want our lives to count for the display of his greatness. Work in us to this end with all your might, we pray. In Jesus' name, amen.

"Like the lightning,

when it flashes out of one part of the sky,

shines to the other part of the sky,

so will the Son of Man be in His day.

But first He must suffer."

LUKE 17:24-25

✤

The Lord Jesus will be revealed

from heaven with His mighty angels

in flaming fire.

2 THESSALONIANS 1:7

✤

13

THE APPEARING OF THE GLORY OF OUR GREAT GOD AND SAVIOR

The Second Coming of Jesus Christ

✤

A t his first coming, Christ partook of flesh and blood so that "through death he might render powerless him who had the power of death . . . and might free those who through fear of death were subject to slavery all their lives" (Hebrews 2:14-15). He will appear a second time to save those who are eagerly waiting for him (Hebrews 9:28).

The time is coming when faith will be swallowed up by sight. For now, "we walk by faith, not by sight" (2 Corinthians 5:7). But at the last trumpet, when the dead are raised and we are changed in the blink of an eye (1 Corinthians 15:52), spiritual and physical seeing will coalesce into one overwhelming apprehension of the glory of Christ.

For now, we "see" Christ with the "eyes of [the] heart" (Ephesians 1:18). God shines in our hearts to give us the "light of the gospel of the *glory* of Christ" (2 Corinthians 4:4, 6). "No one knows the Son except the Father" (Matthew 11:27).

So if we see the glory of the Son, what Jesus said to Peter is true of us as well: "Flesh and blood did not reveal this to you, but My Father who is in heaven" (Matthew 16:17). When that happens, we are "beholding . . . the glory of the Lord" (2 Corinthians 3:18).

But there is a glory to come that we do not now see. Paul calls it our "blessed hope"—"the appearing of the *glory* of our great God and Savior, Christ Jesus" (Titus 2:13). *First* there was the suffering of the Son of Man and the revelation of its glory only to the eyes of faith (1 Corinthians 1:18, 23). *Then*, at the end of the age, comes a glory for all to see with the natural eyes. "Like the lightning, when it flashes out of one part of the sky, shines to the other part of the sky, so will the Son of Man be in His day. But first He must suffer" (Luke 17:24-25).

Glory—this is the way the inspired writers speak of that event again and again. "The Son of Man comes in His *glory*, and all the angels with Him" (Matthew 25:31). Not just some of the angels. *All* of them. "The number of them was myriads of myriads, and thousands of thousands" (Revelation 5:11). Heaven will be left without a single angel.

And when the Son of Man comes, "He will sit on the throne of His *glory*" (Matthew 25:31, NKJV). And from that glorious throne he will reign. "The government will rest on His shoulders. . . . There will be no end to the increase of His government or of peace . . . with justice and righteousness . . . forevermore" (Isaiah 9:6-7).

That glory will be the glory of the Son of Man (Matthew 25:31). But because the Son of Man is also the Son of God and he and the Father are one, it will also be "the glory of His Father" (Matthew 16:27). His coming is simply called "the revelation of His *glory*" (1 Peter 4:13), and every saint, Peter says, will be "partaker also of the glory that is to be revealed" (1 Peter 5:1).

The joy of the saints, who "rejoice with exultation" at his coming (1 Peter 4:13), will be the joy of prizing and praising the unclouded glory of Christ. This is why he is coming—"to be *glorified* in His saints on that day, and to be marveled at among all who have believed" (2 Thessalonians 1:10).

And what will the display of all this glory be? It will be "the voice of the archangel and the trumpet of God . . . the sky . . . split apart like a scroll when it is rolled up, and every mountain and island . . . moved out of their places" (1 Thessalonians 4:16; Revelation 6:14). It will be the fire of judgment. "The Lord Jesus will be revealed from heaven with His mighty angels in flaming fire" (2 Thessalonians 1:7). All nations will be gathered before him, and every unbeliever "will pay the penalty of eternal destruction, away from the presence of the Lord and from the glory of His power" (2 Thessalonians 1:9). Kings of the earth and lowly slaves will hide themselves "in the caves and among the rocks of the mountains" and cry out to the rocks, "Fall on us and hide us from . . . the wrath of the Lamb" (Revelation 6:15-16). "That lawless one will be revealed whom the Lord will slay with the breath of His mouth" (2 Thessalonians 2:8). "Every eye will see Him, even those who pierced Him; and all the tribes of the earth will mourn over Him" (Revelation 1:7).

But the glory of the coming of the Lord will also be salvation. "Christ . . . will appear a second time, not to deal with sin but *to save* those who are eagerly waiting for Him" (Hebrews 9:28, RSV). At "the voice of the archangel and . . . the trumpet of God . . . the dead in Christ will rise first. Then we who are alive and remain will be caught up together with them in the clouds to meet the Lord in the air" (1 Thessalonians 4:16-17).

"By the exertion of the power that He has even to subject all things to Himself" he will transform our disease-ridden, decaying bodies into the likeness of "the body of His glory" (Philippians 3:21). "In a moment, in the twinkling of an eye . . . we will be changed" (1 Corinthians 15:52). "He will wipe away every tear from their eyes, and death shall be no more, neither shall there be mourning nor crying nor pain any more" (Revelation 21:4, RSV).

And perhaps most glorious of all is the jealousy with which he will magnify his grace. He will not share the glory of being the grace-giver. Peter tells us simply, "Fix your hope completely on the *grace* to be brought to you at the revelation of Jesus Christ" (1 Peter 1:13). And what will that grace look like? Jesus pictured it in a parable: "Blessed are those servants whom the master finds awake when he comes; truly, I say to you, he will gird himself and have them sit at table, and he will come and serve them" (Luke 12:37, RSV). It is the grace of God's being our "Servant"—the Giver—even to eternity.

Jesus asked at the Last Supper, "Which is the greater, one who sits at table, or one who serves? Is it not the one who sits at table? But I am among you as one who serves" (Luke 22:27,

RSV). And so it will be to all eternity. Why? Because the giver gets the glory. Christ will never surrender the glory of his sovereign grace. "He [is not] served by human hands, as though He needed anything" (Acts 17:25). He created in order to have beneficiaries who magnify his bounty. And he will bring history to an end as the everlasting Giver. From beginning to end his aim is the same: "the praise of the glory of His grace" (Ephesians 1:6). Come, let us worship and bow down. Let us love his appearing. "In the future there is laid up for me the crown of righteousness, which the Lord, the righteous Judge, will award to me on that day; and not only to me, but also to *all who have loved His appearing*" (2 Timothy 4:8).

A PRAYER

Forgive us, Father, for our indifference to the coming of your Son. We have not kept our lamps of expectation burning or bought the oil of eagerness in hope for the Bridegroom to return. We have bought a field and gone to look at it. We have bought oxen and spent time ooing and aahing over their height and weight. We have married a wife and desired her more than the coming of your Son. O Lord, forgive us. We are sorry for the dishonor that our wandering affections show to you and your servant, Jesus. But, Lord, we are eager to change. And we come to you for help. Incline our hearts to Christ. Open our eyes to the glory of Christ.

Make the appearing of our great God and Savior a "blessed hope" in our hearts—a happy hope, a satisfying hope. Break our addiction to this world. Cause us to set our minds on things that are above where Christ is seated at your right hand. Work in us the command of Peter to "hope fully in the grace of God that is coming at the revelation of Jesus Christ." Free us from the anxieties that come from too much dependence on earthly circumstances. Form us into a radical band of risk-takers in the cause of love because we know that this mortal flesh will put on immortality and this body of lowliness will be transformed into a body like Christ's glorious body. We love you, Father. We love your Son's appearing. Grant us to live out this hope in the freedom of self-sacrifice to the glory of your great grace. In Jesus' name, amen.

CONCLUSION

Getting Right with God Through Jesus Christ

☙

I close with a summary of six truths that may help some readers make the decisive move from alienation from God to reconciliation with God. My hope is that you have seen Jesus Christ and that a spiritual savoring of his glory has been awakened in your heart. Or it may be that you find yourself blocked at the border of faith. In either case, perhaps a summary statement of saving truth from the Bible will make the difference. "Quest for Joy"[1] is a pamphlet I wrote some years ago to help guide people toward a saving relationship with Jesus Christ. It would be my great joy if God used it to solidify your trust in Christ. As I said in the Preface, the quest for well-founded, everlasting, love-producing joy is serious. Everything is at stake. There is no more important issue in life than seeing Jesus for who he really is, and savoring what we see above all else.

> *"Delight yourself in the LORD; and he will*
> *give you the desires of your heart."*
> PSALM 37:4

QUEST FOR JOY

Six Biblical Truths

✣

GOD CREATED US FOR HIS GLORY.

*"Bring My sons from afar and My daughters from the ends of the earth
. . . whom I have created for My glory."* ISAIAH 43:6-7

God made us to magnify his greatness—the way telescopes magnify stars. He created us to put his goodness and truth and beauty and wisdom and justice on display. The greatest display of God's glory comes from deep delight in all that he is. This means that God gets the praise and we get the pleasure. God created us so that he is most glorified in us when we are most satisfied in him. (See Chapter One of *Seeing and Savoring Jesus Christ.*)

EVERY HUMAN SHOULD LIVE FOR GOD'S GLORY.

"So whether you eat or drink or whatever you do, do it all for the glory of God." 1 CORINTHIANS 10:31, NIV

If God made us for his glory, it is clear that we should live for his glory. Our duty comes from his design. So our first obligation is to show God's value by being satisfied with all that he is for us. This is the essence of loving God (Matthew 22:37) and trusting him (1 John 5:3-4) and being thankful to him (Psalm 100:2-4). It is the root of all true obedience, especially loving others (Colossians 1:4-5). (See Chapter One of *Seeing and Savoring Jesus Christ.*)

ALL OF US HAVE FAILED TO GLORIFY GOD AS WE SHOULD.

"All have sinned and fall short of the glory of God." ROMANS 3:23

What does it mean to "fall short of the glory of God?" It means that none of us has trusted and treasured God the way we should. We have not been satisfied with his greatness and walked in his ways. We have sought our satisfaction in other things, and treated them as more valuable than God, which is the essence of idolatry (Romans 1:21-23). Since sin came into the world we have all been deeply resistant to having God as our all-satisfying treasure (Ephesians 2:3). This is an appalling offense to the greatness of God (Jeremiah 2:12-13). (See Chapter Seven of *Seeing and Savoring Jesus Christ*.)

ALL OF US ARE SUBJECT TO GOD'S JUST CONDEMNATION.

"The wages of sin is death." ROMANS 6:23

We have all belittled the glory of God. How? By preferring other things above him. By our ingratitude, distrust, and disobedience. So God is just in shutting us out from the enjoyment of his glory forever. "They shall suffer the punishment of eternal destruction and exclusion from the presence of the Lord and from the glory of his might" (2 Thessalonians 1:9, RSV).

The word "hell" is used in the New Testament twelve times—eleven times by Jesus himself. It is not a myth created by dismal and angry preachers. It is a solemn warning from the Son of God who died to deliver sinners from its curse. We ignore it at great risk. (See Chapter Eleven of *Seeing and Savoring Jesus Christ*.)

If the Bible stopped here in its analysis of the human condition, we would be doomed to a hopeless future. However, this is not where it stops . . .

GOD SENT HIS ONLY SON JESUS TO PROVIDE ETERNAL LIFE AND JOY.

"Here is a trustworthy saying that deserves full acceptance: Christ Jesus came into the world to save sinners." 1 TIMOTHY 1:15, NIV

The good news is that Christ died for sinners like us. And he rose physically from the dead to validate the saving power of his death and to open the gates of eternal life and joy (1 Corinthians 15:20). This means God can acquit guilty sinners and still be just (Romans 3:25-26). "For Christ died for sins once for all, the righteous for the unrighteous, to bring you to God" (1 Peter 3:18, NIV). Coming home to God is where all deep and lasting satisfaction is found. (See Chapters Two, Eight, Nine, and Twelve of *Seeing and Savoring Jesus Christ.*)

THE BENEFITS PURCHASED BY THE DEATH OF CHRIST BELONG TO THOSE WHO REPENT AND TRUST HIM.

"Repent, then, and turn to God, so that your sins may be wiped out." ACTS 3:19, NIV

"Believe in the Lord Jesus, and you will be saved." ACTS 16:31

"Repent" means to turn from all the deceitful promises of sin. "Faith" means being satisfied with all that God promises to be for us in Jesus. "He who believes in me," Jesus says, "will never thirst" (John 6:35). We do not earn our salvation. We cannot merit it (Romans 4:4-5). It is by grace through faith (Ephesians 2:8-9). It is a free gift (Romans 3:24). We will have it if we cherish it above all things (Matthew 13:44). When we do that, God's aim in creation is accomplished: He is glorified in us and we are satisfied in him—forever. (See Chapter Ten of *Seeing and Savoring Jesus Christ.*)

Does this make sense to you?

Do you desire the kind of gladness that comes from being satisfied with all that God is for you in Jesus? If so, then God is at work in your life.

What should you do?

Turn from the deceitful promises of sin. Call upon Jesus to save you from the guilt and punishment and bondage. "Whoever will call on the name of the Lord will be saved" (Romans 10:13). Start banking your hope on all that God is for you in Jesus. Break the power of sin's promises by faith in the superior satisfaction of God's promises. Begin reading the Bible to find his precious and very great promises, which can set you free (2 Peter 1:3-4). Find a Bible-believing church and begin to worship and grow together with other people who treasure Christ above all things (Philippians 3:7).

The best news in the world is that there is no necessary conflict between our happiness and God's holiness. Being satisfied with all that God is for us in Jesus magnifies him as a great Treasure.

"You have made known to me the path of life;
you will fill me with joy in your presence
with eternal pleasures at your right hand."
PSALM 16:11, NIV

A NOTE ON RESOURCES

Desiring God Ministries

❧

If you would like to ponder further the vision of God and life presented in this book, we at Desiring God Ministries (DGM) would love to help you. DGM is a resource ministry of Bethlehem Baptist Church in Minneapolis, Minnesota. Our desire is to fan the flame of your passion for God and help you spread that passion to others. We have hundreds of resources available for this purpose. Most of our inventory consists of books and audiotapes by John Piper. We also maintain a large collection of free articles, sermon manuscripts, and audio messages at our web site. In addition, we produce God-centered children's curricula, host conferences, and coordinate John Piper's conference speaking schedule.

Since money is not our treasure we try to keep our prices as low as possible. And since we don't want money to be a hindrance to the Gospel, if our prices are more than you can pay at this time, our *whatever-you-can-afford* policy applies to almost all of our resources—even if you can't afford to pay anything! We also accept VISA, MasterCard, Discover, and American Express credit cards for convenience and speed, but we would rather give you resources than have you go into debt.

DGM exists to help you make God your treasure. Because God is most glorified in you when you are most satisfied in him.

For more information, call to request a free resource catalog or browse our online store at *www.desiringGOD.org.*

DESIRING GOD MINISTRIES
720 Thirteenth Avenue South
Minneapolis, Minnesota 55415-1793
Toll free in the USA: 1-888-346-4700
International calls: (612) 373-0651
Bethlehem Baptist Church: (612) 338-7653
Fax: (612) 338-4372
mail@desiringGOD.org
www.desiringGOD.org

DESIRING GOD MINISTRIES
UNITED KINGDOM
23 Ashburn Avenue
Waterside, Londonderry
Northern Ireland BT46 5QE
Tel/fax: (02871) 342 907
desiringGOD@UK-Europe.freeserve.co.uk

NOTES

PREFACE (pp. 11-17)

1 C. S. Lewis, *Mere Christianity* (New York: Macmillan, 1952), p. 56.

2 Milan Machove, *Jesus für Atheisten* (Stuttgart: Kreuz Verlag, 1972).

3 F. F. Bruce, *New Testament Documents: Are They Reliable?* (Downers Grove, IL: InterVarsity Press, 1984); Craig L. Blomberg, *The Historical Reliability of the Gospels* (Downers Grove, IL: InterVarsity Press, 1987); Paul Barnett, *Is the New Testament Reliable? A Look at the Historical Evidence* (Downers Grove, IL: InterVarsity Press, 1993); Gregory A. Boyd, *Cynic Sage or Son of God? Recovering the Real Jesus in an Age of Revisionist Replies* (Grand Rapids, MI: Baker Book House, 1995); Gary R. Habermas, *The Historical Jesus: Ancient Evidence for the Life of Christ* (Joplin, MO: College Press Publishing Company, 1996); Michael J. Wilkins and James P. Moreland, eds., *Jesus Under Fire: Modern Scholarship Reinvents the Historical Jesus* (Grand Rapids, MI: Zondervan Publishing House, 1996); Luke Timothy Johnson, *The Real Jesus: The Misguided Quest for the Historical Jesus and Truth of the Traditional Gospels* (San Francisco: Harper, 1997); Lee Strobel, *The Case for Christ: A Journalist's Personal Investigation of the Evidence for Jesus* (Grand Rapids, MI: Zondervan Publishing House, 1998).

4 *The Westminster Larger Catechism*, Question Four. John Calvin describes the "testimony of the Spirit" like this: "The testimony of the Spirit is more excellent than all reason. For as God alone is a fit witness of himself in his Word, the Word will not find acceptance in men's hearts before it is sealed by the inward testimony of the Spirit. The same Spirit therefore who has spoken through the mouths of the prophets must penetrate into our hearts to persuade us that they faithfully proclaimed what had been divinely commanded . . . because until he illumines their minds, they ever waver among many doubts!" (*The Institutes of the Christian Religion*, I, vii, 4, ed. John T. McNeill [Philadelphia: The Westminster Press, 1960], p. 79). "Indeed, Scripture exhibits fully as clear evidence of its own truth as white and black things do of their color, or sweet and bitter things do of their taste" (*Institutes*, I, vii, 2, p. 76).

5 See note 3.

CHAPTER 3 (pp. 35-39)

1 Jonathan Edwards, "The Excellency of Christ," in *The Works of Jonathan Edwards*, vol. 1 (Edinburgh: The Banner of Truth Trust, 1974), p. 680.

CHAPTER 6 (pp. 57-62)

1 See an excellent treatment of the Bible's teaching on the divinity of Christ in chapter 26 of Wayne Grudem, *Systematic Theology: An Introduction to Biblical Doctrine* (Grand Rapids: Zondervan Publishing House, 1994), pp. 529-563.

CHAPTER 8 (pp. 73-79)

1 *Ecclesiastical Histories*, IV, 15, vol. 1, translated by Kirsopp Lake (London: William Heinemann Ltd., 1965), p. 341.

2 Henry Dosker, in *International Standard Bible Encyclopedia*, Geoffrey W. Bromiley, ed., vol. 2 (Grand Rapids, MI: Eerdmans, 1995), p. 761, citing Josephus, *Jewish Wars*, V, xi, 1.

CONCLUSION (pp. 123-127)

1 This pamphlet may be ordered from Desiring God Ministries (1-888-346-4700). If we can be of any help in your "quest for joy," we would be glad.

SCRIPTURE INDEX

✤

SUBJECT INDEX